DogLife ❧ Lifelong Care for Your Dog®

AUSTRALIAN SHEPHERD

tfh

Elizabeth M. Jarrell

AUSTRALIAN SHEPHERD

Project Team
Editor: Heather Russell-Revesz
Copy Editor: Ellen Bingham
Indexer: Elizabeth Walker
Series Design: Mary Ann Kahn and Angela Stanford
Book Design: Mary Ann Kahn

TFH Publications®
President/CEO: Glen S. Axelrod
Executive Vice President: Mark E. Johnson
Publisher: Christopher T. Reggio
Production Manager: Kathy Bontz

TFH Publications, Inc.®
One TFH Plaza
Third and Union Avenues
Neptune City, NJ 07753

Printed and bound in China

12 13 14 15 16   1 3 5 7 9 8 6 4 2

Library of Congress Cataloging-in-Publication Data
Jarrell, Elizabeth M.
  Australian shepherd / Elizabeth M. Jarrell.
     p. cm.
  Includes index.
  ISBN 978-0-7938-3615-4 (alk. paper)
  1. Australian shepherd dog. I. Title.
  SF429.A79J37 2012
  636.737--dc23
                         2011034115

This book has been published with the intent to provide accurate and authoritative information in regard to the subject matter within. While every reasonable precaution has been taken in preparation of this book, the author and publisher expressly disclaim responsibility for any errors, omissions, or adverse effects arising from the use or application of the information contained herein. The techniques and suggestions are used at the reader's discretion and are not to be considered a substitute for veterinary care. If you suspect a medical problem consult your veterinarian.

Note: In the interest of concise writing, "he" is used when referring to puppies and dogs unless the text is specifically referring to females or males. "She" is used when referring to people. However, the information contained herein is equally applicable to both sexes.

The Leader In Responsible Animal Care For Over 50 Years!®
www.tfh.com

CONTENTS

INTRODUCTION

INTRODUCING THE AUSTRALIAN SHEPHERD

Despite the name, Australian Shepherds—commonly referred to as Aussies—are an American breed through and through. Although the history of the breed is largely speculative, it is clear that they were mainly developed in the American West and Midwest starting around the beginning of the 20th century.

HISTORY OF THE AUSTRALIAN SHEPHERD

The history of the breed has been documented by the Australian Shepherd Club of America (ASCA). The club issued two yearbooks of great historical interest about the breed; the first covered the years 1957–1977, and the second addressed the years 1978–1982.

In the first yearbook, Phillip C. Wildhagen, club historian and influential person in the breed, wrote an essay called "History of the Australian Shepherd." He began by pointing out that when early man began to domesticate animals, dogs were domesticated to act as shepherds for the new livestock. Dogs were bred according to a function; in this case, the function was to herd specific types of livestock. The English, Scots, Germans, and Spanish all bred early types of herding dogs. Indeed, among today's dogs, certain breeds and even particular lines within each of these breeds are often bred to herd a particular type of livestock—ducks, sheep, cattle, etc.

In the 1700s, many Europeans immigrated to both the United States and to Australia. Often these immigrants brought their herding dogs with them for assistance in their new country. Although no one knows for sure, it is probable that some of these herding dogs are the early forebears of today's Australian Shepherd. The dogs who accompanied shepherds from Australia were generically called "Australian Shepherds."

There are persistent rumors that Australian Shepherds were developed in the Basque country between France and Spain. Legend has it that some Basque shepherds immigrated to Australia, taking their shepherd dogs with them. In due time, these same Basque shepherds supposedly immigrated to the United States, particularly to the American West, again taking their shepherd dogs with them. Supposedly, these same shepherd dogs were then developed into the forebears of the modern Australian Shepherds.

Aussies use different degrees of "eye," grip, voice, and even body to herd livestock.

Legends aside, dogs in the 19th and 20th centuries earned their keep for the most part, just as they had done in Europe. A herding dog had to be a reliable and dependable worker. Different types of livestock require different skill sets. As a result, dogs who worked in areas where cattle were the predominate livestock were bred to possess the skills sufficient to herd cattle. Similarly, dogs who were used in areas where sheep were the more common livestock were bred to have the skills best used to herd sheep. Different lines of herding dogs resulted, but the one thing they all had in common was the prized ability to be a good herding dog, a good working dog. Eventually, these dogs developed into a single breed—the Australian Shepherd.

As the old saying goes, "A good herding dog should be tough enough to control a belligerent ram yet gentle enough to comfort a newborn lamb." Good herding dogs are born instinctively knowing how to do both. They all use different degrees of "eye," grip, voice, and even body to herd livestock.

Rising Popularity in the United States

By the 20th century, the United States was becoming less of an agricultural country. Big cities were springing up. Dogs were prized as pets, not necessarily for their ability to work livestock. During this time, one man in particular helped make Australian Shepherds more well known (and as a result more popular) in the United States, especially in the northwestern part of the country. His name was Jay Sisler.

Jan Haddle Davis's essay "The Idaho Aussie and Jay Sisler" (from the second ASCA yearbook) explains that in the late 1940s to early 1950s, Jay Sisler trained dogs to perform in a traveling rodeo act. According to Davis, "The Sisler-trained dog act was quite incredible. His Aussies, being so eager to please, would jump rope, stand on their heads, balance on bars, climb ladders, and more." Indeed, Sisler gets credit "for beginning a tradition of great dogs!"

Jay Sisler went on to even greater heights than his amazing rodeo act. Walt Disney Productions contracted with Sisler and his Australian Shepherds to appear in movies. *Cow Dog* was released by Walt Disney Productions on January 16, 1956, starring Slim Pickens, Jay Sisler, and his famous Australian Shepherd "Stub." It was only a 22-minute featurette, but director Larry Lansburgh's short film was nominated for an Academy Award in the Best Short (Live Action Subjects) category in 1956.

The second movie, *Stub: Best Cow Dog in the West*, featured Sisler's dogs "Stub," "Queen," and "Shortie." This 49-minute movie was a "made for television" show created for *The Wonderful World of Disney*. It originally aired December 8, 1974, and was also directed by Larry Lansburgh. Walt Disney Studios Home Entertainment re-released this movie on January 17, 2008, in large part due to petitions from loyal Australian Shepherd owners. The plot involves Sisler's highly trained and

Australian Shepherds were developed in America.

ASCA was organized by and for people dedicated entirely to Australian Shepherds.

fearless Australian Shepherds saving the day by controlling a rogue Brahman bull that was interfering with a valuable herd of pedigreed Hereford cattle.

One thing was clear during this time: Jay Sisler was an incredible ambassador for the Australian Shepherd. He brought Australian Shepherds into people's living rooms, demonstrated their incredible intelligence and athleticism, and began to make the breed known throughout the United States.

MAJOR BREED CLUBS

The two primary breed clubs offering registration privileges to Australian Shepherds are the Australian Shepherd Club of America (ASCA) and the American Kennel Club (AKC). ASCA is unique in that it allows registration privileges for Australian Shepherds only for purposes of obtaining a breed championship. Interestingly enough, ASCA offers obedience and herding titles for all other dogs, purebred or not. The AKC is an organization for the registration of pedigreed dogs for breeds that it recognizes.

The Australian Shepherd Club of America

ASCA was organized by and for people dedicated entirely to Australian Shepherds. The club was officially established as the parent club for the breed and organized as a nonprofit corporation in 1957. Today, the club has over 100 affiliate clubs both within the United States and abroad, including Canada, Great Britain, and Europe.

ASCA is responsible for the written standard for the breed (effective January 15, 1977). The breed standard is the description of the breed against which all individual dogs are judged. In conformation shows, dogs are not judged against each other; rather, dogs are judged against the written breed standard. The ASCA breed standard specifically addresses the following areas: general appearance; character; head, including teeth, eyes, and ears; neck and body; forequarters; hindquarters; color, including disqualifications; gait; and size. These areas will be discussed in greater depth in Chapter 1.

ASCA offers titling events in conformation, obedience, tracking, agility, rally, and of course stockdog. The stock titles can be earned on three types of stock—cattle, sheep, and duck. Each activity has various levels of titles. Shows sanctioned by ASCA are often informal, relaxed, and always fun. Under the new rules, an affiliate club can hold two shows on the same day or four total shows over a weekend. On many weekends, the affiliate clubs offer conformation, obedience, and stockdog events. Sometimes these events take place all at the same time in different areas of the show site. Usually, the people who show enjoy lunches and dinners together. Often, shows have an educational event, such as a grooming seminar, during the lunch or dinner break. The camaraderie evident at these shows is especially welcoming to those people new to the breed.

Once a year, usually around late September, ASCA holds a national event known as the nationals. The location in the United States varies from year to year to give everyone an equal chance to travel to the show site. Invitations are issued to owners of dogs

The AKC officially recognized Australian Shepherds in 1993.

The AKC offers many titling events, including those for conformation.

who have achieved the highest rankings in the areas of conformation, stockdog, agility, and obedience. These types of competitions are called invitationals and are separate competitions for each event to determine the best of the best. Later, there are open competitions for any eligible Australian Shepherd. Nationals are a great place to meet people who are extremely knowledgeable and enthusiastic about the breed. Usually, there are various educational events, for example some relating to health issues. There are also vendors specializing in unique items featuring Australian Shepherds.

The ASCA offers many other benefits to its members, including a subscription to *The Aussie Times*, the official bimonthly publication that has been nominated several times for national writing awards. *The Aussie Times* offers current information concerning national and affiliate clubs, including upcoming events and results of competitions from all over the country. These events are great places to meet people who love Aussies and would prefer nothing better than to spend the day (better yet weekend!) discussing the wonders of Australian Shepherds.

In addition, *The Aussie Times* has regular breed columnists who discuss such topics as training for herding, agility, tracking, and obedience; the status of these various programs; and rescue matters. What makes *The Aussie Times* even more interesting is that several columnists write helpful, often animated stories about these dogs. Members spend many hours discussing the often full-page advertisements for various dogs to understand their bloodlines.

The club also offers educational programs and helps keep the membership current on relevant legislative matters. You can visit their website at www.asca.org.

The American Kennel Club

The AKC was founded in 1884. It is considered to be both the oldest and the largest dog registry in the world. Unlike the ASCA, individuals do not obtain membership within the AKC; however, like ASCA, the AKC registers dogs.

The AKC recognizes over 160 breeds of dogs, which are divided into groups determined in large part by the function for which the breed was developed. Although there has been recent discussion about changing the groups, the current ones are Sporting, Hound, Working, Terrier, Toy, Non-sporting, Herding, and Miscellaneous.

The Australian Shepherd is a member of the Herding Group, which currently has 23 different breeds in it. As the name implies, all the breeds within this group were developed for the common job of herding. The Herding Group was created in 1983, largely out of dogs from the Working Group.

The Australian Shepherd was officially recognized by the AKC to compete in Herding Group events on January 1, 1993. Accordingly, the AKC has a written breed standard for the Australian Shepherd. Their standard specifically addresses the following areas: general appearance; size, proportion, and substance; head, including expression, eyes, ears, muzzle, faults, and disqualifications; neck, topline, and body, including chest and tail; forequarters, including shoulders, legs, pastern, and feet; hindquarters, including stifles and feet; coat, including severe faults; color, including disqualifications; gait; temperament, including faults; and disqualifications. The breed standards of the ASCA and the AKC are very similar. However, there are some highly technical differences. As mentioned earlier, these areas will be discussed in greater depth in Chapter 1.

The AKC holds the AKC/Eukanuba National Championship for conformation, obedience, and agility once a year, usually in early December. Dogs are invited to participate based on their performance throughout the preceding year. In addition to a plethora of interesting vendors, the AKC organizes an educational event called "Meet the Breeds," where experts present their breed and are available to answer any questions.

The Westminster Kennel Club (WKC), an affiliate club of the American Kennel Club, hosts an annual show at Madison Square Garden in New York City every year in the middle of February. This well-known show is open only to finished champions; this means dogs who have already earned their championships. It is also unique in that it is a benched show, where the dogs are kept in an area known as the "benching area" so that spectators and other exhibitors can see them up close. Often their owners are available to answer questions as well. This show is televised and eagerly watched by a national audience.

Anyone, whether or not they have a dog registered with the AKC, can subscribe to the club's magazines, which range from *Family Dog* (geared for pet owners) to The *AKC Gazette* (available online and designed for the more serious breeders). Both magazines offer a wealth of general information about dogs. *The AKC Gazette* also lists events throughout the country, including conformation, obedience, rally, and agility. These large shows are a wonderful way to meet people with similar interests. The American Kennel Club offers many titling events, including those for conformation, obedience, tracking, agility, rally, and stockdog. You can find out more at www.akc.org.

The United States Australian Shepherd Association

The United States Australian Shepherd Association (USASA) is another organization devoted exclusively to Australian Shepherds.

The United States Australian Shepherd Association (USASA) is an organization devoted exclusively to Australian Shepherds.

Unlike ASCA, the USASA does not register individual dogs. Instead, the USASA is the national breed club affiliated with the AKC. Accordingly, USASA Australian Shepherds are registered by and can earn titles from the AKC.

The USASA holds a national competition each spring called the nationals. It is a great place to meet people interested in the breed and who can offer guidance about the breed. There are often educational events at these nationals as well as vendors specializing in items relating to the breed.

The USASA publishes a magazine every other month called *The Australian Shepherd Journal*. Several of their columnists have won national writing awards. The features generally include conformation, tracking, agility, junior showmanship, and rally. The magazine also lists rankings in events such as conformation, obedience, rally, herding, and agility. As with *The Aussie Times*, the advertisements of dogs are invaluable in terms of developing an eye for the breed.

INFLUENTIAL AUSTRALIAN SHEPHERD PEOPLE

ASCA offers special recognition to people who have influenced the breed. In particular, ASCA has both a Hall of Fame program and a newer Hall of Fame Excellent program awarded to named kennels and the people who associated with them. It is a great honor and privilege to be a Hall of Fame or a Hall of Fame Excellent kennel.

The USASA has a similar program called Hall of Fame Breeders. Being a new organization, there are fewer listings. It is, however, also a great distinction to become a Hall of Fame Breeder.

In general terms, all these individuals have contributed greatly to the development and promotion of the Australian Shepherd. The focus is on having bred a certain number of dogs who have achieved excellence in a variety of areas. These areas include conformation as well as performance events such as obedience and agility and, of course, herding. Achieving recognition as a Hall of Fame Breeder requires years of tremendous dedication to the breed.

INFLUENTIAL AUSTRALIAN SHEPHERD DOGS

The ASCA also offers several special recognition programs for special dogs. These programs are the Hall of Fame Sires and Dams; Versatility and Supreme Versatility Championships; and Performance and Supreme Performance Championships. There are detailed rules associated with each of these programs, which mainly deal with achieving a certain number of titles from the categories of conformation, obedience and rally, and performance, including herding events. Australian Shepherds are one of the most versatile dogs, and the ASCA strongly promotes and supports continuing and preserving the versatility of this breed.

In a similar fashion, the USASA also has a few special recognition programs for memorable dogs. In particular, the USASA recognizes Record of Merit and Hall of Fame Sires and Dams. Recognition involves complicated rules but generally requires attaining or producing puppies that attain a specific number of titles within the categories of conformation, obedience and rally, and performance, including herding events. Attaining any of these recognitions deems a dog indeed special.

PART I

PUPPYHOOD

CHAPTER 1

IS THE AUSTRALIAN SHEPHERD RIGHT FOR YOU?

Are you an athletic person? Do you have a wicked sense of humor? Are you willing to spend a lot of time each and every day playing with your dog? Are you an independent thinker who is smart enough to stay one step ahead of a very smart dog? If you answered yes to all these questions, then the Australian Shepherd just may be a good breed for you. There's no one breed that's right for everyone, and Australian Shepherds are no exception.

BEHAVIORAL AND PERSONALITY TRAITS

For fanciers of Australian Shepherds, no other breed can compare, but they are not the right breed for everyone. Aussies are extremely active, very athletic, and highly intelligent (not surprisingly, their owners believe them to be the most intelligent of all dogs!).

Australian Shepherds require a tremendous amount of time and attention from their owners. Some do not stop acting like puppies until they are around three years of age and many *never* stop acting like puppies. Because of this, Australian Shepherds are not likely to spend their evenings sitting on the couch watching TV. They need a job to do, and if their owner doesn't provide one, the Aussie will find something to do on his own. When that happens, the owner may not appreciate the so-called job that their Australian Shepherd decided to do!

Herding Instincts

As a member of the Herding Group, the Australian Shepherd has strong herding and guardian instincts. Instincts are important because they dictate who the dog is; they are part of the dog's genetic makeup. Instinctive behaviors are difficult to train out of a breed and, indeed, it would not really be fair to do so. You may find that your young Australian Shepherd wants to herd your children and their friends, your other dogs, and perhaps even you. Your young pup may take it upon himself to bark or nip to get his point across. Many Australian Shepherds will follow you from room to room—even into the bathroom! They want to be with you; they love to watch you. Between their intelligence and their herding instincts, Australian Shepherds are intense breeds requiring a lot of time and attention.

The Australian Shepherd has strong herding and guardian instincts.

The Aussie's membership in the Herding Group is significant in another way. As mentioned earlier, herding dogs were bred to do a job—in their case, herding livestock. They love nothing better than to work. Unfortunately, more people live in cities and suburbs than out in the country these days, so most dog owners do not have ready access to livestock for herding. The good news is that Australian Shepherds are highly trainable, incredibly intelligent, and one of the most versatile of all breeds. They can learn just about anything, and most are enthusiastic about learning. So even if you can't give an Aussie an official herding job, you can find other things for him to do. Aussies excel at dog sports such as obedience, rally, agility, and flyball. There are many training clubs all over the country that can help get a new owner started.

Active and Athletic

Tremendously active dogs, Australian Shepherds must receive both mental and physical exercise each and every day. A daily walk is a must, and a rousing round of catching tennis balls, especially for a puppy, is also helpful. After that, your Aussie is ready to learn. A ten-minute daily training session is enough. It doesn't matter what you train your dog to do—even training a few tricks gives him the mental workout he needs. Providing this type of physical and mental exercise on a daily basis is an absolute must and requires a time commitment by the owner.

Their athleticism means that Aussies can (almost literally) turn on a dime. They can jump into the air, turn 360 degrees in one direction while in the air, land, and then jump back into the air and turn 360 degrees in the opposite direction—all in a matter of seconds. Australian Shepherds are tremendous natural jumpers. This makes them excellent in such activities as obedience and agility. However, it also means that they can quite casually leap obstacles such as short backyard fences.

Biddable

Aussies are often described as "soft," as opposed to "hard," dogs. Soft dogs are very connected to their owners; they really and truly want to please them. Indeed, this attribute of sincerely desiring to please their owners, called biddability, is one of the hallmarks of the breed. This biddability, together with the breed's almost unparalleled athleticism, is what makes them so versatile. Competitive performance enthusiasts highly prize such versatility.

Another trait of soft dogs like Aussies is that they do not understand harsh or unfair corrections. In fact, they tend to stop working when confronted with such training methods.

Devoted

Whatever an Australian Shepherd does, he does with his whole heart. They are tremendously engaged with and devoted to their owners. If an owner loves a particular activity, such as obedience, most often an Australian Shepherd will love doing that activity simply out of devotion to his owner.

Aussies are super smart, and you'll have to be one step ahead of them at all times.

Intelligent

Australian Shepherds are super smart. You have to think one step ahead of them all the time. As smart herding dogs, Australian Shepherds are hard-wired to think independently. They will make decisions on their own unless guided by you to do otherwise.

Playful and Happy

As former rodeo dogs, Aussies have an innate sense of humor. They love to play and have fun. Most of all, they love to have fun with their owners, whom they adore. Some will even steal socks just to get their owners to play with them!

Since Australian Shepherds in America have docked tails, they are known among their owners as "wiggle butts." This is because most Australian Shepherds wiggle their butts in utter delight whenever they are happy and usually when they meet people, even strangers. While the vast majority of Aussies are intense dogs, they can be happy-go-lucky as long as they are given sufficient physical and mental daily exercise.

Reserved

Australian Shepherds can be what is described as reserved when first meeting strangers. They do not necessarily bound up to everyone they meet. But they should never, ever act aggressively toward anyone at any time—not even to strangers. An aggressive dog is a poorly bred dog; such behavior is completely unacceptable. If someone describes a dog as "sharp," it is often a euphemism for aggressive.

Snorts, Smiles, and Aussie Talk

Part of their fun-loving nature includes several unusual but endearing characteristics. The first is their snorting, which by no means indicates that they have respiratory problems—rather, it is how Australian Shepherds laugh. While your Aussie is cavorting away with your stolen socks, he will in all likelihood be snorting. Yes, your Australian Shepherd is actually laughing at you. When two Aussies are playing together, you will always know it is just play when they are snorting happily at each other.

The second prized characteristic of most Aussies is their smile or grin. In its strictest sense, both smiling and grinning are gestures of submission. The dog is telling the person or other dog that he is not a threat. Australian Shepherds often smile when they are happy. Many an Aussie owner comes home to his dog smiling back at him, happy to give a huge welcome. Grinning is nothing more than more pronounced smiling. When a dog grins, he pulls back his lips and exposes teeth. Sometimes only the front teeth are shown, but often the side teeth are also displayed. Grinning dogs are not snarling; it is a submissive, not an aggressive, behavior.

Another delightful attribute of Australian Shepherds is that they often talk. Talking is also a submissive behavior, although to the untrained eye, it may appear to be aggressive growling. Nothing could be further from the truth. Aussies may make low, grumbling noises, commonly referred to as "talking." Some also grunt, groan, squeak, squawk, or just make generalized sounds. Many a happy Australian Shepherd talks when supremely happy. Some will even grab a toy and start talking with the toy in their mouth—more than a few choose to greet visitors in this way. Needless to say, it is fairly easy to teach an Australian Shepherd to speak on command; it is not so easy to teach them to be quiet!

Stimulation

Most of all, Australian Shepherds love to spend time doing activities with their owners. They need to go out and about, see new people, and go to new places. They love riding in the car. They need constant daily stimulus or else they become easily bored, and a bored Aussie is all too often a destructive Aussie. All an Australian Shepherd wants most in life is to be doing something active with his owner; they thrive on being on the go with their loved ones.

PHYSICAL CHARACTERISTICS

Both the Australian Shepherd Club of America (ASCA) and the American Kennel Club (AKC) have exact breed standards that go into great depth about every important physical

Aussies need constant daily stimulus.

The Aussie's double coat provides insulation against extremely hot and cold temperatures.

characteristic of the Australian Shepherd. However, for the purposes of this book, I will present a general description of the breed's physical characteristics, including size, coat type, color, general body structure, legs, feet, movement, head and neck, bite, eyes, and ears.

Size

In general, males are about 20 to 23 inches (51 to 58 cm) at the withers (the point of the shoulder). Females are slightly smaller; they are around 18 to 21 inches (46 to 53 cm) at the withers. An Aussie's weight should be in proportion to the height. With such a wide range in height, Australian Shepherds can weigh anywhere from about 40 to 60 pounds (18 to 27 kg).

Coat Type

The Australian Shepherd has what is known as a double coat. This means that there is a longer, heavier topcoat on the outside and a shorter, fluffier undercoat on the inside closer to the skin. The undercoat is what insulates the dog, which is very important. As with other double-coated breeds, the coat insulation protects the dog from extreme heat and cold. Some owners might be tempted to shave their Aussie's coat, but shaving removes the undercoat and the dog's natural insulation against extremely hot and cold temperatures.

A proper coat on an Australian Shepherd is weather resistant—this means that the coat is semi-waterproof. For moisture to penetrate their protective undercoat, these dogs must be absolutely soaked to the skin. In addition, when an Aussie gets muddy (and many love to play in the mud), the dirt falls off as it dries (usually around the house). A good Australian Shepherd coat acts like a good Oriental carpet: It sheds dirt naturally once dry.

Australian Shepherds shed but only from the undercoat. (If your Aussie is losing his topcoat, then that is a sign of ill health.) Losing the undercoat is called *blowing coat*. Typically, intact females will shed their undercoats twice a year right before coming into season. Males, whether intact or not, drop their undercoats about once a year, usually when winter arrives. Because of its insulating properties, dogs in colder climates tend to grow more undercoat than do dogs in warmer climates.

The texture of the coat is straight to slightly wavy. If there is any slightly wavy hair, it usually appears on top of the back between the hips. Often puppies have slightly wavy hair that goes away after their first major shed (around one year of age). A positively curly coat is deemed a severe fault in the show ring.

This breed carries a coat of medium or moderate length overall. However, the length of the coat depends on where it is located on the body. The coat on the head, outsides of the ears, front of the front legs, and below the hocks on the back legs is smooth and short. The coat on the back of the forelegs develops moderate feathers or longer hair. The coat on the top of the back legs develops moderately fuller feathers known as *britches*. The back of the neck grows a moderate mane, which then

What Is a Hock?

A hock is the joint on the back leg of a dog that bends backward and roughly corresponds to the human ankle joint but is higher up.

Multi-Dog Tip

Since Australian Shepherds come in four different colors, you can have your pick of looks. These colors are black tri, blue merle, red tri and red merle all with or without copper and/or white. Whatever color you prefer, the colors should be rich on a well-bred Aussie

circles the entire neck and is known as *frill*. Aussies tend to be almost three years of age before they develop full feathers including those on the back of the forelegs, britches, mane, and frill.

Males generally carry much more coat than females. Their topcoat tends to be longer, and their undercoat tends to be thicker. And, as mentioned above, males are not subject to loss of coat due to coming into season, which occurs on average about twice a year for females. Males will, however, shed once a year.

Color

One spectacular characteristic of Australian Shepherds is that they can be one of four different colors—all of which should be strong and rich, never unacceptably dilute. The acceptable colors are black, blue merle, red, and red merle. A merle is a speckling of shades with spots ranging in size. The blue merle has gray spots, and the red merle has red spots. All four colors can have white markings, usually around the collar, feet, and belly. Similarly, all four colors can have copper points (highlight patches) generally on the cheeks and eyebrows. White body splashes other than in these areas are disqualifications for showing. The area

One spectacular characteristic of Australian Shepherds is that they can be one of four different colors.

around the eyes and ears should be dominated by a color other than white and show pigment.

The black and blue merles have black pigment on the nose and lips, whereas the reds and red merles have liver pigment on those areas.

General Body Structure

Since the Australian Shepherd is a herding dog, the general body structure should be sufficient to permit the dog to work all day long. Everything about the dogs' appearance goes back to their function as a herding dog. The overall key to their structure is moderation and balance, because these are the qualities that allow a herding dog to do his job. In overall appearance, the dog should be slightly longer than tall. The body should be firm and well muscled.

In terms of substance, the dog's bone, which means its thickness (especially the leg bones), should fit the dog's height. Australian Shepherds should not look clunky; neither should they look overly weedy. Further, the boys should look like boys, and the girls should look like girls.

Legs

The forequarters and hindquarters each have angles. These angles should be about the same in order to present an overall balance of the outline. A sound dog is a balanced dog able to cover ground quickly and effortlessly. A dog with uneven, overly steep, or overly shallow angles is not as efficient a mover. A dog whose front angles do not match his rear angles, and vice versa, may even be more prone to injuries, as one half of the dog is working harder than the other half to compensate for the unequal angulation.

Feet

Feet are very important to all herding dogs. At the end of the day, a herding dog is only as good as his feet; if he has bad feet, he cannot do his job. The Australian Shepherd's feet should have thick pads. The overall shape of the feet should be oval, with tight, arched toes.

Movement

This is a *movement breed*, meaning that these dogs are bred to move effortlessly and in a balanced fashion. The front legs should reach forward, and the rear legs should drive backward. Further, the dog's reach and drive should be roughly equal so as to maintain balance.

As with other herding breeds, the Australian Shepherd tracks when moving at the appropriate speed at a trot, with trotting being the most efficient gait. Roughly translated, tracking means that the back right leg fills the invisible hole left on the ground by the front right leg. Likewise, the back left leg fills the invisible hole left on the ground by the front left leg. When these legs almost meet in the middle, you should be able to imagine a triangle of sorts made by the feet and the bottom line, defined below.

The *topline* (area on top of the dog's back) should remain level when trotting. Some Australian Shepherds lower their head at a trot. The *bottom line* (area under the belly between the legs) has a moderate tuck up. The import of all of this is that you should be able to see balanced, easy movement on an eight-week-old

To own an Aussie, you should have and enjoy a very active lifestyle.

puppy. Such movement is an indication of a sound, well-balanced dog, which itself is a sign of sound structure.

Head and Neck

Generally speaking, the Australian Shepherd's head should fit his body. There are several styles of head that are acceptable, but all head styles should be clean and in proportion to the body. The dog should not look like he has a head as big as a steering wheel. The lips should be tight, with clean lines. This is not a drooling breed.

The top of the head can be level or slightly domed. If you look at the head from the side, the length of the area of the nose should roughly equal the length of the area of the top of the skull. The area where these two parts meet is called the *stop*, and it should be moderate. The muzzle can be a bit tapered but never snippy.

The neck is a critical part of any dog's anatomy. It should be strong, moderate in length, and show some arch at the top. It is important that the neck meets the shoulders well.

Bite

Australian Shepherds should have a scissors bite, with the top teeth slightly scissored over the bottom teeth and the upper incisors located precisely in front of the lower incisors when the mouth is closed. They should not be missing teeth.

Eyes

This breed has exceptionally expressive eyes. You should be able to tell what an Australian Shepherd is thinking and feeling by looking into his eyes. The Aussie's intelligence shines through the eyes as well. Their eyes should be shaped like almonds, not circles, and they

Often, the merles have one eye in each color.

should not protrude. A dog with round bug eyes is more likely to be injured by a kick from a cow or a sheep. The pupil should be dark, centered, and well defined.

Another striking attribute of Australian Shepherds is their eye color, which may be blue or brown. Often, the merles have one eye of each color. It is possible, although rare, for the blacks to have one or two blue eyes. In addition, each eye may be two different colors. Some merles have eyes with flecks of another color.

Ears

In this breed, the ears are placed high on the side of the head. The ears should not be set low, as you see on certain hounds. The shape of the ears is triangular, with some rounding at the tip. The end of the ear should be able to touch the inside corner of the eye. When the dog is alert, the ear should fold slightly forward and rise about one quarter to one half of its length above the base. The ears should not stand straight up, which is known as *prick ears*. Ears that look houndy (droopy) or prick are severe faults in the show ring.

DOES THE AUSTRALIAN SHEPHERD FIT INTO YOUR LIFE?

It is important to discover if an Aussie will fit into your life, so that both you and the puppy are happy together. To do so, you should consider the Aussie's needs in terms of environment; amount of exercise; sociability with respect to strangers, children, and other dogs and pets; grooming; health; and trainability.

Want to Know More?

How to socialize a puppy will be discussed in Chapter 4: Training Your Australian Shepherd Puppy.

Environmental Needs

The Australian Shepherd needs a lot of land so he can run. If you do not have sufficient land, then you must be dedicated to several long walks every day. Aussies do not do well in city apartments— they need too much daily physical exercise to live in most cities. They will do fine in a suburban area, provided you walk them sufficiently. Of course, they positively thrive in open rural areas.

It is ideal (and fairest to the Aussie) if you have a back yard; it is mandatory that you have a good fence as well. Most Australian Shepherd owners have 6-foot (2-m) stockade fencing which prevents the dogs from jumping the fence and also from seeing the neighbors and any of their dogs. Aussies (as well as many other breeds) will run the fence line barking at neighbors' dogs when they can see them. A stockade fence mostly solves this problem.

Exercise Needs

The key to a happy Australian Shepherd is a lot of daily physical activity, and a happy Aussie is a good Aussie. People living in the suburbs who work full time can have well-adjusted Australian Shepherds, but these owners must provide at least two daily walks of at least 1 mile (2 km) apiece. In addition, daily rounds of throwing tennis balls in the back yard are important—especially for puppies. Your yard will get a lot of use, so if you have your heart set on a green back yard with lush grass, consider another breed.

Some Australian Shepherds are more active than others; however, relative to other breeds, the Australian Shepherd is considered to be very active. To own an Aussie, you should have and enjoy a very active lifestyle. If you do not currently have an active lifestyle, you surely will after getting your Australian Shepherd puppy.

Sociability

Well-bred Australian Shepherds are social creatures, but they need daily socialization through at least their first year. And it is in their best interest to continue their socialization after that time—in other words, there is no such thing as an overly socialized puppy. As is the case with many herding breeds, some Australian Shepherd puppies tend to be a bit shy when first meeting strangers or when confronted with new situations and places. Most will get over this and become more outgoing the more you socialize them. Socialization is absolutely mandatory to have a well-adjusted Australian Shepherd.

With Children

Australian Shepherd puppies need an enormous amount of time, attention, and devotion from their owners. People with children under six are usually already exhausted from dealing with their children and may not have any time or energy left to socialize an Aussie puppy. Generally speaking, Australian Shepherds do best in households

Most Australian Shepherd puppies can easily be raised with other dogs.

with children who are at least six years of age. Children younger than that, especially toddlers crawling on the floor, may be "herded" by young Australian Shepherds. If you do have a toddler in the home, your best bet if you get a puppy is to train him while he's still young that herding babies is not acceptable. It is possible to raise young children together with Australian Shepherd puppies, but it requires extra vigilance on the part of the adults.

With Cats

Some Australian Shepherds may try to "herd" other pets, like cats. The key to living happily with an Aussie and cats is the same as with toddlers—introduce the puppy to the cat when he is extremely young, and do plenty of early training.

With Dogs

Most Australian Shepherd puppies can easily be raised with other dogs. If you have only two dogs, it's a good idea to get one of each sex; they tend to like each other more. Generally speaking, the girls tend to be dominant over the boys, and there are fewer arguments about status.

If you bring a puppy into your home and you already have a dog, the puppy should never be left alone with the adult dog. An adult dog could accidentally hurt a puppy. An adult Australian Shepherd is a powerful dog that could, without meaning to, slam into a puppy and break his leg. Plus, some adult dogs just do not like puppies, so you need to be sure that your dog will accept one before bringing one home.

For similar reasons, an Australian Shepherd puppy brought into a household with a toy dog should always be watched when they are together. By sheer weight alone, once your Australian Shepherd grows into an adult, he could accidentally hurt a small dog.

Grooming Needs

Australian Shepherds have gorgeous coats in signature colors. But this is not just a coated breed—this is a *double-coated* breed. Australian Shepherds shed, and when they do, there are balls of hair all over the place. In other words, this breed requires grooming.

In general, an Australian Shepherd should be groomed once a week. If you start grooming your Aussie while he's a puppy, he'll get used to it and hopefully learn to enjoy these times together. Your weekly grooming sessions will include:

- Clipping nails: Nails must be kept short to keep the dog's feet and legs healthy. Overly long nails make a dog walk awkwardly, overly stressing and, over time in extreme cases, possibly even breaking down the legs. If you have a dog, you must clip his nails once a week.

Get your puppy used to grooming right away.

One of the hallmarks of this breed is its trainability.

- Combing down to the skin: Australian Shepherds should be combed down to the skin to prevent hair mats and skin issues from developing. In addition, any hair that you remove with a comb is that much less hair scattered all over your house. You should first spray water on the coat to prevent breakage, especially of the hairs in the topcoat.
- Brushing teeth: You should do this at least once a week. You must use toothpaste specially formulated for dogs, which is readily available at most pet stores. There are doggie toothbrushes, but you can also simply wrap a large gauze pad around your index finger, squirt a little dog toothpaste on the pad, and get to work.

One thing you won't need to do weekly is give your Aussie a bath. Since a proper Australian Shepherd coat sheds most dirt when it's dry, it does not generally smell or need many washings. However, you should give your puppy a few baths so that he gets used to the idea and learns to accept it.

In addition to making him more beautiful, these grooming sessions should be bonding events. Your puppy should learn to love being handled and groomed by you. As your dog gets older, you can take advantage of these grooming sessions by evaluating his overall health.

Health Issues

Perhaps because this is a relatively new breed, Australian Shepherds overall are a healthy breed and tend not to have too many health issues. If, however, you suspect that your puppy may have one of the health issues listed below, you should take him to your veterinarian for a complete examination.

Hip dysplasia is a problem that impacts the rear legs. In hip dysplasia, the hip socket is not formed tightly. Hip dysplasia is more noticeable in older dogs than in puppies. Signs can range from mild lameness to becoming unable to move. Some dogs with hip dysplasia never show any symptoms. Some cases can be managed through maintaining proper weight, but others require surgical intervention up to and including a complete hip replacement.

As with other herding dogs, Australian Shepherds can have several inherited eye problems. They can have coloboma, which means that the eye is not properly formed. Some colobomas result in only mild impairment of the eye; others may result in blindness. Another potential inherited eye problem is a cataract, which may occur while the dog is still very young or may show up later in life. As with coloboma, a cataract may cause only mildly impaired vision, but it could also result in blindness. Some cataracts can be completely removed through surgery.

Another rare disease found in Aussies is epilepsy, which causes the dog to have seizures ranging from mild to extreme. Unfortunately, there is no easy cure for epilepsy. Certain drugs may help to manage the disease in some cases.

Training Tidbit

Start training your Australian Shepherd puppy as soon as you get him home, but keep your training sessions very short and make them lots of fun. Always end on a positive note, letting your puppy be successful.

Trainability

One of the hallmarks of this breed is its trainability. Australian Shepherds are a joy to train. They can be trained to do just about anything the owner is willing to take the time to do. Indeed, Australian Shepherds positively thrive on training. It provides them mental exercise that they require on a daily basis. The more training you provide, the happier and healthier your Australian Shepherd puppy will be. Training also helps build the relationship between you and your young puppy. If you enjoy training, then it is almost certain that your puppy will too. At the end of the day, all any puppy wants to do is engage with his owner.

CHAPTER 2

FINDING AND PREPPING FOR YOUR AUSTRALIAN SHEPHERD PUPPY

Do you love adorable balls of fluff? Are you a patient person? Are you willing to spend a lot of time keeping a close eye on a puppy? Are you active enough to keep up with a very rambunctious puppy? Are you patient enough to train a puppy? If so, then maybe you are a good candidate for an Australian Shepherd puppy.

There are many decisions to make before you get a dog. One of the first is whether to get a puppy or a full-grown adult. Other decisions include getting a conformation dog for the breed ring or a nice companion to be your family pet. Then you'll have to find a breeder, which involves learning what to expect from a breeder, finding out what documents are required, and fully understanding any guarantees the breeder may offer.

THE ADVANTAGES OF GETTING A PUPPY

After deciding that the Australian Shepherd is the perfect breed for you, it's time to decide if you want to get a puppy or an adult dog. There are advantages and disadvantages to each.

A puppy is truly a blank slate; he knows nothing of the world. He also knows nothing about what types of behavior are acceptable. A well-bred puppy delights in meeting new people, going to new places, seeing his first flower, and just basically enjoying everyday life. Simply put, a puppy's enthusiasm about being alive is contagious—you cannot help but be equally excited about being alive yourself.

Puppies, and especially Australian Shepherd puppies, are very silly about just about everything. They continually play and amuse themselves and their owners. You will spend many happy hours laughing along with your funny puppy. Often, your puppy will smile and snort (his way of laughing) right back at you. Everything is new and exciting to a puppy; the world is his oyster.

However, a puppy knows absolutely nothing about how to behave properly. Your puppy, especially during his first year, will require a total commitment from you, as you are the one who must teach him how to behave in this new world. You must be willing to socialize and train the puppy, and he will need much more of both than an adult dog will. A puppy lovingly raised by you is likely to become the adult dog you desire, because you are the one who taught him how to act properly.

You'll have to decide between a pet-quality and a show-quality puppy.

PET OR SHOW-QUALITY?

Most breeders sell two types of puppies: show-quality puppies and pet-quality puppies. On average, puppies go to their new owners at eight weeks of age, which many believe is the perfect time to see how the puppy's conformation or structure will look as a mature adult. When a breeder calls a puppy a "show" puppy, the breeder is essentially saying than in her opinion, based on her years of experience, this particular puppy's conformation looks likely to be good enough to be used as a breed dog when he grows up. No breeder can predict that any one puppy at eight weeks will indeed grow up to be a champion show dog. All a breeder can do is give you her best guess.

Sometimes, there are immediate disqualifications to an otherwise perfectly structured puppy. In the Australian Shepherd, one of the most common such disqualifications has to do with color. For example, a puppy with a head that is half white would be disqualified in a breed show based on his color. Another example of a color disqualification would be a puppy who is marked like a pinto pony. There is absolutely nothing wrong with these "pet-quality" puppies. They are simply not showable in the breed ring. The good news is that a "pet-quality" puppy will be less expensive than a show-quality puppy.

WHERE TO FIND THE PUPPY OF YOUR DREAMS

There are several different places to find the Australian Shepherd puppy of your dreams, but the best place is a reputable breeder. This is a person who loves the breed and is passionate about what she does in order to improve the breed. Such a breeder is networked with other similar breeders to stay current on the latest information regarding these dogs. A good breeder will become your friend and your mentor and help you find the resources you may need throughout the life of your puppy. You may even in time become part of the breeder's network and acquire much valuable information about Australian Shepherds over the many years of your connection with her.

Breeding Is Hard Work

A healthy and happy litter of puppies is absolutely delightful, but a litter is also a tremendous amount of work on the part of the breeder.

The time and effort on the part of a breeder from the time the litter is whelped to the time the puppies leave at around eight weeks of age is beyond comprehension unless you too have bred and raised a litter. To begin with, birthing, or whelping, a litter can be stressful to the mother dog and to the breeder. Whelping does not occur on a set schedule. Often dogs have

Breeding healthy dogs takes a tremendous amount of work.

puppies in the quiet of the middle of the night. If there are problems, such as a puppy stuck in the birth canal, the mother must be rushed to the emergency vet.

The mother keeps her puppies clean, but the breeder must keep the bedding clean. Many breeders have to do a full load of laundry every day for the entire eight weeks to make sure the puppies always have clean bedding.

By the time the puppies reach eight weeks, the amount of time, energy, and attention that both the mother and the breeder have devoted can be overwhelming. It is then time for the puppies to be placed in good homes. At about eight weeks, it is better for the puppy to be in a new home, with a new owner devoted exclusively to raising and bonding with

him. An entire book could be written on the subject of the trials and tribulations involved in finding the right person for each puppy. Screening potential puppy buyers is a full-time job in and of itself.

Leaving Mom

Why does the breeder keep the puppies until they are about eight weeks old? Many states have laws concerning the minimum age that a puppy must be before a breeder can allow that puppy to leave his mother. When states have such laws, the average age ranges from about seven weeks to maybe even nine weeks. These laws exist to protect the puppy. Young puppies need their mother for many things—not just nutrition. Mother dogs are nature's best puppy

If a breeder does not know you personally, you can expect her to interview you about your suitability for one of her special puppies.

Avoid Puppy Mills

Of late there has been a resurgence of puppy mills. Breeders from puppy mills are completely disreputable. You do not want to purchase a puppy from them. You should also avoid stores that may have bought puppies from a puppy mill.

teachers. The mother has much to teach her puppies before they are ready to leave the nest.

One of the most important things a mother teaches her puppies is the beginning of socialization. She teaches them how to get along with her and also with their littermates. All that squawking you hear when in the presence of a litter of puppies is the puppies learning how to get along with each other. The mother keeps a close eye on their activities. She never lets them get out of hand, so their playing together never turns to fighting.

The mother also teaches her puppies the beginnings of bite inhibition. The mother does not permit her puppies to bite her. She also does not permit her puppies to bite each other. Puppies taken too soon from their mother may never learn proper bite inhibition.

Finding a Breeder

Before you start looking for a breeder, you should ask yourself what you want to do with your puppy. Some people want a particular type of show dog for a certain venue—perhaps conformation or breeding, obedience or agility. Other people most emphatically want a nice pet. After deciding what you want to do with your new puppy, you then have to find a breeder who specifically breeds or has bred that type of puppy. Many breeders breed dogs suitable for all show venues, but you need to ask them what their dogs have accomplished.

The conformation ring is designed to showcase excellent conformation examples of the breed. The point of a champion is that the dog's conformation meets the breed standard.

Most breeders show their dogs to get their breed championships before breeding them.

Therefore, one of the best places to find a good breeder is at a dog show. Infodog (www.infodog.com) is a website devoted to informing the public about the dates and locations of dog shows, including breed, obedience, and agility. Search Infodog to find a dog show near you, and go watch the show. Make sure that you are there at the right time and at the correct ring for Australian Shepherds. If you are more interested in an obedience or agility dog, use Infodog to find obedience and agility shows near you. While watching, be mindful that the exhibitors are

Allow your breeder to help you choose the right puppy for you.

busy getting ready to show or compete with their dogs. Most breeders will be happy to talk with you—but only after the show is over.

Both the Australian Shepherd Club of America (ASCA) and the United States Australian Shepherd Association (USASA) maintain a list of breeders by state. Neither club endorses any of these breeders, but the lists are a great starting point. Many breeders have websites that are included on these lists. You can locate a breeder near you, identify shows near you, and then call the breeder and ask to meet her at the show.

If a breeder does not know you personally, you can expect her to interview you about your suitability for one of her special puppies. The breeder will ask you many questions, some of which will most likely include the following:

• Have you ever owned a dog? If so, how many

and how long did the dog(s) live?
• Do you have children? If so, how many and what ages?
• Do you have any other pets? If so, how many and what type?
• Do you have a fenced yard?
• Do you work at home? If you work in an office, do you keep fairly regular hours?
• Do you want to show your puppy or have someone else show him for you?
• Do you have any references, which could include your vet?

You can then ask the breeder any questions you may have. Some of your questions might include the following:

• How long have you had Australian Shepherds, and how long have you been breeding them?
• How many champions have you produced?

- How many dogs have you bred that earned obedience, agility, or other performance titles?
- What health checks have been done on the parents?
- What guarantees do you offer?
- Who are your references from other breeders or those to whom you have previously sold puppies?
- Are the mother, the father, or any close relatives available for you to meet?

Paperwork and Guarantees

You also need to ask the breeder if the litter is registered with the ASCA, the USASA, or both. If you would like to register your puppy, then you should ask if you will receive the registration papers for both national clubs. For a small fee, you can then register your new Australian Shepherd with both breed clubs.

The breeder should also provide a three-generation pedigree. You can ask for pictures of both parents. Most breeders will allow you to photograph the litter as a memento.

Another important question is to ask what, if anything, the breeder guarantees. This is determined by the various health checks that were performed on the parents. Guarantees vary widely. At a minimum, most reputable Australian Shepherd breeders have checked the parents' eyes and hips; accordingly, most of these breeders will guarantee a puppy's eyes and hips. While the actual terms can differ, a common guarantee is that if at the age of two, the puppy's eyes or hips are bad after being examined by the appropriate veterinary specialist, then the breeder will take back the puppy in return for the original purchase price and registration papers.

Choosing a Puppy

As for the all-important question of which puppy you should actually take home, the very best thing to do is allow the breeder to choose your puppy. A good breeder has spent the past eight weeks with the puppies. She knows them

far better than you do at that point. Once you explain what you want to do with your puppy and what your living situation is, the breeder will happily select the best puppy for you.

BEFORE YOUR PUPPY COMES HOME

You have quite a lot of work to do before you bring your new puppy home. First, you need to puppy-proof your home and yard. Second, you have to set up a schedule. Last but not least, you need to get all the necessary puppy supplies.

Puppy-Proofing Your Home and Yard

Puppies are extremely curious, and Australian Shepherds—because they are highly intelligent—tend to be even more curious. This curiosity can get them into trouble and is the reason you have to carefully and systematically puppy-proof your home and yard. Puppy-proofing means that you make doubly sure that your puppy cannot get into any physical trouble in your home or yard.

The most important thing you need to do throughout puppyhood is keep a vigilant eye on your mischievous puppy at all times—whether he's out in the yard or in the house (unless he is crated). Puppies should earn house privileges; they should never, ever be left alone in the house to roam about and run amuck. You can make sure that your puppy remains in view by using strategically placed baby gates around the house. If you want to stay in the living room watching television,

Make sure your yard is puppy-proofed before you bring your Aussie home.

then use baby gates to secure the doors so that the puppy is not able to leave that room.

Speaking of the house, Australian Shepherd puppies have a special fondness for the kitchen—they love food. They can be incorrigible counter surfers who routinely sweep kitchen counters in hopes of catching some food. Especially in their first year, remember not to leave any food on the kitchen counter; the same goes for the coffee table.

Any wires, such as those from television sets or computers, should be barricaded away from the puppy. For some reason, teething puppies have a radar lock onto most wires. The more expensive the machine to which the wire is attached, the more diligent the puppy is in finding and chewing the wire. This is not safe for the puppy and does no good for your television set or computer either.

By the age of four months, an Australian Shepherd puppy is perfectly capable of leaping over the back of the sofa and even clearing the coffee table in the process. Clear away any breakables around the house at least for a year. This will prevent you from losing any cherished family heirlooms and will also make the puppy safer.

You also need to puppy-proof your yard. Your veterinarian can provide you with a list of poisonous plants, or you can find lists on the web. If you have any poisonous plants, find some way to prevent your puppy from eating them.

As briefly mentioned earlier, it is simply a must to have a 6-foot (2-m) stockade fence. Check your fencing on a weekly basis to make sure that all boards are secure. Make sure that your gate is shut every time you let the puppy outside. If you have help mowing the grass or raking leaves, make doubly sure that you check the gate on days that your help has been in the yard.

Car Tip

It's a good idea to place a card on the crate in the car with your name and address, your puppy's name, your veterinarian's name, and another contact's name in case of emergency. Also clip a spare leash to the crate.

Setting Up a Schedule

Puppies, especially smart puppies, thrive on a set schedule. So you need to figure out and even write down a schedule for your new puppy. Puppies like to wake up and go to bed at the same time every day. They also like to eat, go potty, go for walks, and enjoy playtime and training time on a schedule. Once you determine your puppy's schedule, post it on your refrigerator door.

If you work full time away from the house, you will need to find someone to let your puppy outside to go to the bathroom in the middle of the day. Puppies simply cannot wait all day. and it is not very nice to ask them to do so. Veterinarians can offer you the names of licensed pet walkers in your area. To select a pet walker, first invite her to come to your home. Then ask her a few questions to see if you can work together. Make sure you know exactly when the pet walker will be visiting every day and how long the visit will last. Also, make sure you understand the applicable fee arrangements.

One of the great benefits of setting up a schedule is that it makes housetraining your new puppy much easier. Housetraining requires consistency on your part. A typical housetraining schedule will look something like this.

Take your puppy out:
• When the puppy first wakes up, including if

Puppies thrive on a set schedule.

he wakes up during the night.
- After the puppy finishes eating and again about 15 minutes later.
- On the hour, every hour, while awake and playing.
- Right before bedtime.
- Anytime the puppy starts circling, which most dogs do as a prelude to going to the bathroom.
- Whenever the puppy asks to go outside.

Supplies

In general, supplies for puppies should not be of the expensive variety. Puppies grow so quickly that they end up outgrowing some items. Plus, once they start teething, which begins at around ten weeks, they tend to chew on a lot of these supplies anyway.

Baby Gate

As mentioned in the puppy-proofing section, you will need one or more baby gates to contain your puppy within a designated space with you. This will enable you to keep a constant eye on your new puppy to keep him out of trouble—if you are fast enough.

Collar and Leash

Since puppies grow at amazing rates, an expandable, flat nylon collar is a wise choice. Both the length and the width of the collar must change as the puppy ages—an eight-week-old puppy needs a ¼-inch (6-mm) width, and an adult does well with a 1-inch (25-mm) width. As for length, most collar widths are available only in certain set lengths, so you can choose the collar based on width.

However, make sure that the collar fits as the puppy continues to grow. You should be able to put two fingers under a well-fitting collar.

A nylon leash matching the collar will work perfectly fine for your Aussie puppy. Leather is delicious to teething puppies; nylon is less tempting and a better choice at this stage. A 6-foot (2-m) nylon leash will be useful for daily walks and for training purposes. Be mindful of the weight of the clip on the leash.

It is your responsibility to know when a puppy should and should not wear a collar. The most important thing about a collar is that a puppy should absolutely *never be left alone wearing a collar*. A puppy should never be left outside in the back yard unattended anyway but certainly not while wearing a collar. It is all too easy for a collar to get hooked onto something and choke the puppy. Another important thing to note is that a puppy should always be wearing a collar when you take him anywhere.

Crate

Having a crate is an absolute necessity; crate training is equally necessary and will be discussed in Chapter 4. Dogs are den animals. The crate should be viewed as a den, not as a place where the dog is sent for punishment.

Adult Australian Shepherds fit into medium-size crates. All a puppy needs is enough room to turn around easily, stand up, or stretch out; therefore, puppies need smaller crates. If a puppy is in too big of a crate, he will tend to soil one corner. You can, of course, buy multiple crates as the puppy grows. However, certain manufacturers are now making crates that can easily be adjusted to allow for more space as the puppy grows. These adjustable crates make ideal choices for your Aussie.

A puppy needs a solid, metal crate. While collapsible nylon crates are marvelous for trained, adult dogs, you can be sure that a puppy will quickly chew his way through them. They are not for puppies. When the puppy becomes more mature, you can put a nice, fluffy crate pad in his crate. For now, old towels will serve you better.

You should purchase several crates. Of course, you need a crate in your home for your puppy to sleep in, and most people chose to

Adjustable, flat nylon collars are a wise choice for a growing puppy.

Teach your puppy to allow you to pick up his bowl while he is eating. Simply pick up the bowl, say "Good puppy," drop in a treat, and return the bowl to him.

have the puppy sleep in their bedrooms. If you have a big house, you may want another crate for, say, the living room. You will also want a crate for traveling in your car. A crate is the safest way for a puppy to travel. In the event of an accident, a solid crate will protect your puppy and may even save his life.

Dog Bed

Whether or not to allow your puppy on your bed and other furniture is a personal decision. The important thing is to make that decision and then be consistent about it.

Either way, most people offer their puppies a special dog bed. Because puppies have accidents and are big-time chewers, find a washable dog bed in a durable fabric. Fleece is one fabric that is available but can be too hot for some puppies in the summer months. If the dog bed has a cover, it should be removable for easy washing.

Food and Water Bowls

Bowls come in a variety of materials—ceramic, plastic, and metal. An Aussie puppy will delight in chewing up a plastic bowl, so metal or ceramic is the best choice. Do be careful about ceramic, though, as some of them may be toxic. Metal is nonbreakable and easily washable, and is the preferred choice among most Aussie owners.

Many Australian Shepherd puppies delight in swimming in their water bowls. For these puppies, a special water bowl is in order. There are several different types of water bowls specifically designed not to tip over easily. Some puppies also love to carry their bowls

Metal bowls are the preferred choice for most dog owners.

around the house, particularly when empty. In my experience, they tend not to do this as much with metal bowls.

Always make sure that the food and water bowls are washed after every meal. Some puppies become attached to their own food and water bowls. For these puppies, make sure that you buy an extra set and switch them around. Also, it is a good idea to have a spare set in the car.

General Grooming Supplies

Unless you are or plan to become an exhibitor, you can do well with moderately priced grooming supplies.

- For nail care, you will need a clipper and styptic powder to use in case of clipping the nails too short. Alternately, some people prefer using a nail grinder.
- For dental care, you will need gauze and dog toothpaste.
- For coat care, you will need a pin brush and comb.
- For overall trimming, you will need medium-size scissors and thinning sheers.

How to groom your puppy will be addressed in Chapter 3: Care of Your Australian Shepherd Puppy.

Toys and Chews

A hallmark of Australian Shepherd puppies is that they simply adore toys. They love nothing better than engaging you in play with their toys; they love playing with other dogs and

Curious Aussie puppies love to play with toys.

Give your puppy safe toys to chew on.

teach your puppy to engage actively in playing with you. This can become a great bridge to training later. Fleece tug toys are especially popular with Aussies.

Chews are another important item to give your puppy. Puppies need to chew. Their gums are hurting, and chewing not only relieves the pain, it helps the teeth to emerge. There are many schools of thought as to which chews should be given to puppies. As with toys, do not leave your puppy alone with chews.

Chews are available in many different materials. Nylabone has a line of safe chews designed specifically with puppies in mind. In view of recent problems with imported dog products, check the country of origin for whichever chews you give your puppy.

BRINGING YOUR PUPPY HOME

You will always remember with great fondness the day you bring your puppy home. Make sure you have a camera to capture that special day. Bring your puppy home early on a Saturday so that you can have the weekend to get to know each other a bit.

You may want to ask your breeder if she could let your puppy sleep alone in a crate on

their toys; they even love playing alone with their toys. However, no puppy should be left unattended with toys. Puppies become teething machines at ten weeks of age and can accidentally eat their toys, resulting in dire consequences.

There are a wide variety of toys available from many retailers. Many Australian Shepherd puppies love to sleep on top of plush toys—using them as pillows. They especially like plush toys with squeakers, but be watchful that they do not pull out the squeakers and eat them.

Many Aussie puppies love to play fetch. Tennis balls are great for fetch because they are too large for even most Aussie adults to accidentally swallow. You will go through many tennis balls playing fetch every day in your back yard with your puppy.

Tug toys are excellent choices because they

By the Numbers

Teething begins at about ten weeks and continues until the puppy is about ten months. During this time, a puppy will be a voracious chewer. If you do not provide him with something suitable to chew, he will surely find something himself.

his last day there—this will make his transition to being in a crate much easier. Another good thing to request of your breeder is to put a collar on your puppy. This way, the puppy will be slightly used to wearing one. If your breeder is especially cooperative, ask her to also introduce the puppy to a leash. Last, ask your breeder to not feed your puppy before you leave. This will make the ride home much more enjoyable for all of you.

Your puppy should be crated in the car, not held in your lap. The crate is a far safer place for your puppy while riding in a car. Remember to put on his new collar and leash before you take him out of the crate. Your puppy has no idea that this is his new home. Plus, no dogs should be outside without a collar and leash anyway. The minute you arrive home, put

your puppy on the grass and ask him to do his business. The motion of the car will almost certainly have caused him to want to produce the desired results. Then allow him inside.

Introductions

Your new home may be overwhelming to your puppy. Go slowly and be relaxed about his introduction to his new home.

If you have small children, allow them to meet the puppy one at a time. Hold the puppy on your lap, and let each child gently pet the puppy. The children should not run around shouting because they will terrify your Aussie puppy. You also need to show small children how to pick up the puppy and explain that they should do so only when you are there to watch. Another important point is to teach

Teach children to only pick up the puppy when an adult is present.

your children to leave the puppy alone when he is eating or when he is sleeping. This is for everyone's safety. Similarly, if you have other dogs, let them meet the puppy individually. The same applies to other animals, such as cats. Never leave the puppy with small children or other animals unless you are there and actively supervising their interaction.

Next, show him his water bowl. Make sure you put in fresh water. After that, show him his new crate. Then, just enjoy your new puppy!

The First Night

If your breeder crated the puppy the night before, then your puppy's first night in the crate at home will go much easier. If not, then expect that the puppy will be vocal about his objections to being crated. Make sure the puppy has eliminated just before you crate him for the night. Then, ignore him if he barks and otherwise carries on about being crated. Some puppies calm down within minutes; others take what seems like forever. There are puppies who go to sleep and then wake up in the middle of the night their first night; these are puppies who might need to go to

Your new home may be overwhelming to your puppy.

the bathroom. Put on his collar and leash and take him outside. When he is finished, promptly and quietly put him back into the crate for the rest of the night. If not, you will be spending much time outside in the middle of the night.

The Vet

At the first possible moment, take your puppy to your vet for a complete physical examination. Many breeders will give a buyer two days within which to take the puppy to the vet. If the vet determines that the puppy is extremely ill or unfit temperamentally, the puppy may be returned.

WHAT TO EXPECT THE FIRST FEW DAYS AND WEEKS

Eight-week-old Australian Shepherd puppies are a wonderful combination of angels and devils all rolled up into an adorable fluff ball. They can be absolutely delightful; they can also be totally exhausting. Keep this combination in mind, and both of you will enjoy puppyhood together.

Want to Know More?

Puppy's first checkup will be discussed in Chapter 3: Care of Your Australian Shepherd Puppy.

At first, your puppy will be on "party manners." He will not put a foot wrong. As he becomes more comfortable, he will start testing you to see if you set any limits. The more comfortable he becomes, the more he will test you.

It is for this very reason that you should enroll in a local puppy kindergarten class and begin attending as soon as possible. Now is the time to find one and get your puppy into the class. There are often wait lists for the best classes.

The first few weeks are important in that you are familiarizing your new puppy with his new schedule—the one you posted on your refrigerator door. The more you stick to this schedule, the happier both of you will be.

This is also the time when you will introduce your dog walker, if you need one, to the puppy. This is an important introduction as well. Ask the dog walker to come to your house, and pay her for this time. See how she interacts with your puppy. Your presence during their initial meeting helps the puppy know that the dog walker will be part of his daily life and is a good person.

CHAPTER 3

CARE OF YOUR AUSTRALIAN SHEPHERD PUPPY

Puppies require a tremendous amount of care, especially during their first year and, in particular, during their first four months. And you are entirely responsible for your puppy's care, including feeding him, grooming him, and making sure that he is healthy. The good news is that the time you spend caring for your puppy gives both of you a chance to bond and develop a strong and special relationship. The more time you are together with your puppy, the stronger your bond will be with him.

Any time you have some doubt regarding how to care for your puppy, it is always a good idea to consult your veterinarian. For general questions, you may even be able to simply call your veterinarian on the telephone and talk to her about the issue. For regular clients, some vets now even offer help over email.

FEEDING YOUR PUPPY

Feeding your puppy involves two major decisions. First, you need to decide what type of food to feed him. Second, you must develop a feeding schedule for your puppy, including how many times a day and exactly what times of the day you will feed him.

The other important part of feeding is to monitor the amount you feed your puppy. Although there are many different opinions on what type of food is best, everyone agrees that making sure your dog is at the proper weight throughout his life is one of the healthiest things you can do for him.

What to Feed Your Puppy

It is always a good idea to ask your breeder for a week's worth of whatever food your puppy has been eating. Many people simply continue feeding their new puppy what the breeder has already been feeding him.

Some people prefer to feed an adult food to puppies who are eight weeks and older. The main differences between most puppy food and adult food are that puppy food generally is higher in protein and has added vitamins and minerals. Those who choose to feed their puppy adult food believe that the slightly lower protein content will allow their puppy to grow at a slow and steady pace. Some maintain that puppies who grow too quickly may develop growth-related issues involving their bones, ligaments, and tendons. In any event, the decision about whether to use a puppy food or an adult food should be made in consultation with your veterinarian.

Feeding Schedule

Remember when you wrote down that housetraining schedule for your puppy and posted it on the refrigerator? Well, now it's time to write down a feeding schedule for your puppy and put it on the refrigerator next to your housetraining schedule. The two, after all, are interrelated; what goes in must come out!

Maintaining a regular feeding schedule is critical for housetraining purposes. If your puppy eats at the same times every day, he will then eliminate at about the same times every day. That's how he becomes accustomed to eliminating on a set schedule.

How Many Times a Day, When, and How Much?

The number of times you feed your puppy and the amount you feed your puppy should be discussed with your veterinarian. Australian Shepherd puppies grow quickly. At the age of eight weeks, most already weigh about 9 or 10 pounds (4 or 5 kg), with the males often weighing more than the females. The key is to feed your puppy enough to grow at a healthy rate without overfeeding him.

Most Australian Shepherds adore their food (in fact, if an Australian Shepherd declines a meal, you should take him to the vet immediately). Many Australian Shepherd puppies will overeat given half a chance. For this reason, as well as for housetraining purposes, you should not free-feed your puppy. Free-feeding means allowing your puppy to eat as much as he wants throughout the day. In addition to promoting obese puppies, free-feeding tends to cause puppies to develop into picky eaters. A good rule is to set your puppy's food down for about 15 minutes. After 15 minutes, pick up the food until the next scheduled feeding. Your puppy will soon

The main differences between most puppy food and adult food are that puppy food generally is higher in protein and has added vitamins and minerals.

Since Australian Shepherd puppies are one of the more active breeds, some owners wait one hour after strenuous activity before feeding their puppies.

learn to eat during those 15 minutes. This will also be invaluable if you decide to travel with your puppy.

A lot of people with Australian Shepherds recommend feeding puppies three times a day until they are four months old (i.e., breakfast, lunch, and dinner). After they reach four months of age, feeding twice a day is sufficient (i.e., breakfast and dinner). It's best to feed at the same time every day and at about the same times as most people generally eat these meals. Some experts believe that feeding in this manner will help prevent bloat, a condition where the stomach may twist and can cause death.

Since Australian Shepherd puppies are one of the more active breeds, some owners wait one hour after strenuous activity before feeding

their puppies. They also wait one hour after eating before permitting the puppy to be so active once again. This helps your puppy to be calm when eating and also have enough time to properly digest his food.

The amount that your Aussie puppy should be fed will obviously increase over time. You can tell if you are overfeeding your puppy because he will look fat—puppies should not have pot bellies. A good rule of thumb is that you should be able to feel the puppy's ribs if you gently press your fingers against his side. As a safeguard, every time you take your puppy for vaccinations, your veterinarian will weigh him. This will allow you to get a feel for whether or not you are feeding the right amount. The best thing you as an owner can do for your puppy (and later as an adult dog) is to keep him at a good weight. This point cannot be overemphasized!

Treats

Treats are an important training tool, which we will discuss further in Chapter 4. However, using too many treats is an easy way to make your puppy fat. Try to find treats that are low fat—there are low-fat cookies and other types of commercial treats available. Puppies do not know the difference between an entire cookie and just a small piece of a cookie; there's no need to give an entire cookie every time you offer your puppy a treat. Small tidbits will equally delight him and be just as effective. By doing so, you won't increase his overall nutritional daily intake too greatly with the addition of too many treats.

Begging

Some people, when they are eating at their table, allow their dogs to beg for food tidbits; others do not. Whatever you decide, once you make a decision, you need to stick

to it. You must be consistent about all your training, including whether or not you will permit your puppy to beg. However, a word of warning is in order—many an Australian Shepherd puppy will stare mournfully up at you with big puppy eyes and perhaps even drool while you are eating. It's a hard act to resist!

GROOMING YOUR PUPPY

Grooming a puppy is very important. Grooming affords you quality time to bond with your puppy. Go slowly and gently so that your puppy learns to love being groomed. You can also talk to your puppy and tell him that grooming is a special time with you.

The process of grooming also is a great way to make sure that your puppy is healthy. If you close your eyes and run your fingers over your puppy's body, you may be able to notice if he has ticks that you otherwise might not see. You can also tell if he has any lumps or bumps that require veterinary attention. If you look closely at his nail beds (where the nail attaches to the skin), you can see if they are infected. Basically, grooming is a good way for you to see or feel if there is anything out of the ordinary going on with your puppy. As a bonus, a puppy who is trained to be groomed will do better when he goes to the vet or if you elect to send him to a professional groomer.

A pin brush is an important tool for brushing your Aussie.

Most people groom their Australian Shepherds once a week. Adults take about 30 minutes, but your puppy does not yet have a full coat, so it will take less time. Australian Shepherds generally do not need to be bathed more than once a month (if that). Bathing takes less than 30 minutes, but blowing the dog dry can take equally as long, if not longer.

Grooming Supplies

There are many different grooming supplies available, and there's a wide range of quality. Unless you plan to show your dog in the breed ring, you do not need the most expensive grooming supplies. For most Australian Shepherd owners, the middle-grade quality of grooming supplies is adequate.

- You will need a comb. Many people prefer combs with teeth of equal length that are evenly spaced through the length of the comb. An easy comb to use is one that has teeth about 1 inch (3 cm) long. Any shorter, and you cannot comb through all the hair; any longer, and you might accidentally comb (and scratch) the skin.
- Another important tool is the pin brush, which is a brush with pins stuck in a pad. The pins should be about 1 inch (3 cm) long.
- For nail care, you have a choice. You can use clippers or a grinding tool. Grinding tools are electric or battery operated. Most people prefer the electric grinders, because they are generally more powerful.
- As for washing your puppy, you have many options for shampoo and conditioner. Human shampoos and conditioners are formulated for human hair, which has a different acidity, or pH level, than that of dogs. So it is best to buy products made for dogs. You may find that you need different shampoos for different colored hair. Some people buy brightening shampoo to use on white areas and then use a regular shampoo for the rest of the body. Also, you may want a special shampoo during the winter, as home heat tends to dry out the skin and coat.

- A grooming table complete with an arm and loop, which help keep your puppy on the table, is an optional but useful purchase. The table will raise the puppy to the height of a regular dining room table and help to save strain on your back. However, if you use a grooming table, never leave your puppy on it unattended. Also, the first time you put your puppy onto the table, give him a few treats to make a pleasant association.

Training Your Puppy to Accept Grooming

A good way to begin is to view grooming as a training exercise. You should be matter of fact about the whole thing and especially gentle at

Get your puppy used to being touched all over his body.

first. Above all, you should act confident about the entire process. Puppies sense when you are insecure, which will make them insecure. The more confident and matter of fact you are about grooming, the easier your puppy will accept it.

Any well-socialized puppy from a good breeder will, for the most part, readily accept being groomed; most actually enjoy it. For those who do not, you must begin very slowly. Gently touch one part of your puppy's body—such as the top of his back—with the brush or comb, and then give him a special treat. Then gently and lightly pull the brush or comb through his hair in the direction in which the hair grows, away from his body. Work your way over the puppy's entire body, treating as appropriate. If the puppy objects, just do one part of the puppy's body each day over the course of a week and gradually, over time, work your way up to grooming his entire body at once.

Brushing and Bathing

Brushing and bathing your puppy is the same as for an adult dog. See Chapter 6 for step-by-step instructions on how to perform these grooming tasks.

Be mindful when you first wash your puppy that you do not get any shampoo in his eyes. That could leave a bad impression on a youngster and create difficulties the next time you wash him.

It is also critical that you be careful if you decide to blow-dry your puppy's coat. The noise and strong air blowing out of the dryer can often scare a young puppy unaccustomed to being blow-dried. At first, you may have to blow-dry just a little bit at a time and let

Want to Know More?

For detailed grooming instructions, including brushing, bathing, and nail care, see Chapter 6: Australian Shepherd Grooming Needs.

the rest of his body air-dry. In time, you can work your way up to blow-drying the entire puppy. The benefit of blow-drying the coat is that it can prevent dampness from perhaps creating skin issues, especially in hot and humid climates. When your puppy grows, he'll have such a thick coat that you would be wise to invest in a blow-dryer designed for dogs, which is far more powerful than those made for people.

Nail Care

Even a well-socialized puppy may object to having his nails clipped. Nail care is an essential part of grooming that should be done on a weekly basis. It is especially important to act in a confident and calm manner when trimming nails. It is equally important not to go too fast at first. For very difficult cases, you may have to trim just one nail a day over the course of a week or more. Be sure to offer a good treat after you trim that one nail. Over time, you can gradually try to trim two nails a day, and work your way up to trimming one entire foot and then all four feet at one time.

Puppies (much like adult dogs), have a special fondness for peanut butter, which can work well as a nail-trimming treat. Give your puppy a taste of peanut butter before you begin. Use peanut butter as a treat only for getting nails done—that way, it will remain a prized treat for your puppy.

PUPPY HEALTH ISSUES

There is nothing sadder than a sick puppy. To prevent this from happening, you need to be aware of certain basic puppy health issues. One of the first is finding the right veterinarian.

How to Find a Veterinarian

Your relationship with your new vet is very important; she will become your new best friend (next to your new puppy, of course). So it is important to find a vet who is knowledgeable and whom you trust and feel comfortable with.

To find a vet, you should first ask your breeder for recommendations. If your breeder lives far away, ask neighbors or friends whom they use for their pets. Some cities have magazines with a consumer guide to various local services, including veterinary services. You can also look up local dog clubs and ask them for a referral. It is much better if you can find a veterinarian who does not live far from you—this way, in case of an emergency, you can get there much faster.

When you find a vet you are interested in, interview her to make sure you think she is sufficiently qualified and that the practice is right for you. Ask the following questions: How long have you been practicing? What are the office hours? Do you have evening and weekend hours? What are the fees? Are credit cards accepted? Do you have payment plans for extraordinary medical expenses? How many people are on staff? Is another veterinarian on hand in case you are not available? How long does it normally take to get an appointment? Will my dog be seen the same day in case of an emergency? What are your scheduling practices? Can I make appointments electronically via email or your website? Do you offer additional services, such as grooming and boarding?

During the interview, you can get a feel for the veterinarian's personality and if you would work well together. You will also be able to see if the facilities are clean and if there is enough room for patients in the waiting room.

If the vet you choose is a bit of a ride from your home, also locate the closest emergency veterinary hospital so that you are prepared in the event of an emergency. Many emergency veterinary clinics ask that you call ahead to allow them to be ready to receive your pet.

Your relationship with your puppy's vet is very important.

Puppy's First Checkup

A well-socialized puppy from a reputable breeder should not have any difficulties with his first checkup. Some breeders even require that a new owner take the puppy to a vet within the first week to make sure that there are no serious health issues.

You may want to bring a stool sample to your first visit. Simply take a plastic bag with you and accompany your puppy outside on the last bathroom visit before leaving for the vet. You may want to double-wrap the sample. The veterinarian will test the sample for any evidence of worms.

The first thing many vets do is weigh the puppy—sometimes by holding the puppy and weighing themselves together, then deducting the vet's weight from the total. This will be a base mark of your puppy's weight for his next visit.

The vet will then put your puppy on the examination table. She will examine his ears (including the inside); open his mouth and look at his teeth; pick up each foot; and gently touch the puppy all over his body. In addition, the vet will listen to your puppy's heart and lungs. The idea is that the vet, like you, wants to get the puppy used to being touched all over in the event that he may later need medical attention on some particular part of his body, or in general just so being touched is a pleasant experience for the puppy and allows anyone who touches your puppy to do so more safely. You may even want to bring some treats with you to the exam. Ask your veterinarian to give your puppy a treat now and then throughout his examination. These treats will help reinforce the idea that going to the veterinarian is a pleasant experience.

The vet will ask you questions regarding your puppy's eating and bathroom routines and how he is doing with socialization. She will also ask if your puppy has any problems that you've noticed. After the initial examination, your veterinarian will discuss general health care, including worm prevention, how to recognize if your puppy is sick, and the typical vaccination schedule. You should feel free to ask her questions at any time.

Puppy Vaccinations

Vaccinations are injections of bacteria or viruses that cause the immune system to make antibodies against that disease. A mother's milk carries some antibodies that give puppies some natural immunity. This is especially true of the initial milk (*colostrum*) that is produced in the first few days after birth. However, this initial immunity decreases over time; a vaccination helps boost that immunity.

A puppy's immune system is not as strong or developed as that of an adult. For this reason, most puppies receive an initial series of puppy vaccinations. These shots are spread out a few weeks apart to allow the puppy's immune system to react sufficiently. Thereafter, a puppy needs to be vaccinated only every so often with a booster shot.

There are two types of vaccinations. The first type uses the killed or otherwise inactivated form of the disease. This is the least effective

Specialists

Modern veterinary medicine has almost as many specialties as does human medicine. There are board-certified veterinarians in the fields of reproduction, dermatology, and the like. If you need a veterinary specialist, your regular vet will recommend one and make the referral for you.

type of vaccination and consequently is given several times over the puppy's and adult's life. The second type uses a modified live virus, where the virus is modified to be less potent. While more effective than the killed type, the modified live virus is more likely to cause adverse reactions.

You should be aware of any signs in your puppy of adverse reactions after a vaccination. The mildest reactions are low-grade fevers and general lethargy. However, in the most severe cases (which are quite rare), reactions can include a full-blown allergic reaction. After receiving a vaccination, if your puppy starts to swell by the injection site or anywhere else on his body (including his face), go immediately to your veterinarian or an emergency veterinarian clinic. Thereafter, your veterinarian may ask you to administer an antihistamine in a predetermined dose prior to receiving a vaccination. Some people choose to vaccinate their puppies against one disease at a time, which spreads out the vaccinations, thereby decreasing the likelihood of any adverse reactions.

The Current Vaccination Controversy

When, how often, and what to vaccinate against is a highly controversial subject. Not too long ago, there was a standard protocol for puppy vaccinations; a majority of veterinarians agreed on which diseases to vaccinate against and when to administer the appropriate vaccination. Today, different protocols exist for both puppy and adult vaccinations. Some owners are even choosing not to vaccinate at all—not even for puppies—because they believe that vaccinations compromise the dog's immune system. However, this approach may not be in your dog's best interest, as unvaccinated dogs run the risk of contracting or dying from a disease that could have been prevented with appropriate vaccination. For this reason, the vast majority of dog owners decide to follow the current standard protocol for puppy and adult vaccinations. This is a matter to discuss at length with your veterinarian—you may even get some input from your breeder.

One way some pet owners avoid over-vaccinating is to titer their adult dog's blood once the dog has received the standard course of vaccinations and is over two years old. This process involves drawing a small amount of blood from the dog and then analyzing it to determine the amount of antibodies in it. If the dog has sufficient antibodies, the veterinarian may advise against a booster for that particular disease until the next year. Also, many people elect not to give booster shots to senior dogs who may not have much contact with other dogs and who may have compromised immune systems.

Diseases to Vaccinate Against

There is much debate among veterinarians and also breeders concerning vaccinations, both for puppies and for adults. The majority of veterinarians recommend vaccinating your puppy against certain diseases. Most commonly, these "core" vaccinations include distemper, canine hepatitis, and parvovirus. (Although parainfluenza is not considered a

A puppy receives some natural immunity from his mother.

core vaccination, it is often included as part of the combination vaccine that includes distemper and parvo.) Additionally, all states require you to vaccinate your puppy against rabies and further require you to administer a booster against rabies to your adult on a scheduled basis.

While some vaccinations are considered to be core vaccinations, others are viewed as elective. For example, some vaccinations are necessary depending only on where you live, such as the one for Lyme disease. Show dogs may also need some of these optional vaccinations, even if the diseases are not necessarily found where you live, as the show dogs are around many dogs from other parts of the country on a frequent basis.

Bordetella

Bordetella, commonly known as kennel cough, is a highly contagious disease contracted through the air. It is most likely that a dog will get bordetella when in close physical contact with other dogs. For this reason, many boarding kennels request that you vaccinate your dog against bordetella prior to boarding him. The usual symptom is a cough that may persist for weeks. In more severe cases, the cough will sound like a honk. Some dogs may also have a discharge from their eyes and nose.

If you see any evidence that your dog may have bordetella, take him to your veterinarian. The veterinarian may treat your dog with antibiotics or other medication. In some cases, the veterinarian may decide that your dog will likely recover without further intervention.

The bordetella vaccination is considered to be an elective, not core, vaccination. It is usually given through the nose of the dog but may sometimes be administered by injection. The vaccine can be given as early as 4 weeks of age but usually isn't given until 8 to 12 weeks of age. The veterinarian will administer two vaccinations, given a few weeks apart and then repeated annually. There are various strains of bordetella, so a bordetella shot may provide protection only for some strains but not for all of them. That's why it is possible that a dog vaccinated against bordetella can still contract the disease, because the shot did not protect against the particular strain to which he was exposed.

Coronavirus

Coronavirus is a virus that attacks the upper respiratory system and gastrointestinal tract. The disease spreads from feces and can be found in the feces of infected dogs for quite some time. Symptoms appear quite quickly. An infected dog may vomit, have diarrhea, and act depressed and lethargic. The feces may also contain mucus and blood and often smells bad. Young puppies are especially susceptible to coronavirus. Infected puppies, even if they do not exhibit symptoms, may be more likely to contract parvovirus.

If you see any of the symptoms, take your puppy immediately to the veterinarian. She may give your puppy medication for the diarrhea or may determine that intravenous fluids are required. The vaccination against parvovirus may also protect against corona. Using disinfectants around the house and keeping your yard free of feces may help prevent this and other diseases.

Distemper

Distemper, prevented by another core vaccination, is extremely contagious and can often be fatal. This disease is caused by a virus and is spread through fluids from an infected dog's nose or eyes. The virus can survive for only a very short period outside of the dog's body and is easily killed by most

Distemper, prevented by a core vaccination, is extremely contagious and can often be fatal.

disinfectants. In addition to dogs, some wild animals may carry the distemper virus.

The symptoms of distemper include a thin yellow to green discharge from the eyes and nose, a loss of appetite, vomiting, diarrhea, fever, coughing, and weakness in the limbs up to actual seizures. The pads on the nose and feet may become thicker. If you see any of these symptoms, immediately take your puppy to the veterinarian.

The vaccination is given to puppies between six to eight weeks old and is then given every two to four weeks until they are four months old. After that, they need a booster at one year of age. A booster may then be given either annually or once every three years. Puppies are much more likely to get distemper than are adults, but distemper can be fatal at any age.

Leptospirosis

The vaccine for leptospirosis is elective. Leptospirosis is actually a family of related bacterial infections stemming from the bacterial group known as *leptospirosis*. These bacteria can lead to infections of internal organs, especially the kidney and liver. Untreated leptospirosis can seriously damage these organs as well as the blood and can even cause death.

The disease is transmitted though contact with urine; infected standing water may also contain leptospirosis. For this reason, it is a good idea never to let your puppy or adult drink or swim in stagnant water. Many people never let their dogs drink from communal bowls, such as those at various training facilities. Another issue is that currently, the vaccination for leptospirosis protects only against certain strains.

The symptoms of leptospirosis are different depending on which particular bacterial infection the dog contracts. These symptoms may include unusual drooling, vomiting, diarrhea, difficulty walking or even the refusal

Lyme disease is more common in certain parts of the country than in other parts.

to move at all, lethargy, fever, dehydration, and shivering. The presence of leptospirosis is confirmed through a blood and urine test for antibodies and bacteria. The treatment will vary depending on the strain involved and may include antibiotics and intravenous fluids.

Lyme Disease

Lyme disease is another disease for which the vaccination is elective. The disease is caused by the bacteria *Borrelia burgdorferi*, which is transmitted by the bite of certain deer ticks. Deer ticks are extremely small and often hard to find, and they can bite people as well as dogs.

This disease is more common in certain parts of the country than in other parts. It was first discovered in Lyme, Connecticut, which is where it got its name. Heavily wooded areas favored by deer are more likely to harbor ticks carrying the disease.

The symptoms of Lyme disease may not appear for several months after the dog has been bitten. When they do appear, they may appear quickly. The symptoms may include high fever, swelling of the joints and lymph glands, general lethargy, and loss of appetite. One very common symptom is lameness that comes and goes.

Early detection is very important in helping to prevent this disease from becoming chronic. The presence of Lyme disease is determined by a blood test. If the test is positive, it can mean either that the dog has Lyme disease or that the dog has been exposed to it and has developed antibodies to the disease.

The treatment usually involves a 30-day course of antibiotics. However, if a puppy is treated for Lyme disease and he has not yet gotten all his adult molars, the antibiotics may discolor any subsequent teeth. Because this disease can become chronic, many believe that a dog that had Lyme disease is more likely to

Removing a Tick

If you find a tick on your dog, as soon as possible use tweezers to remove the tick by grasping as close to the skin as you are able. Use a steady, gentle pull without jerking or twisting. You may want to place the extracted tick into alcohol to kill it, or flush a dead tick down the toilet. You may also want to clean the area on your dog's skin with soap and water, and then dab it with a topical antibiotic.

contract arthritis and at a relatively early age.

The Lyme vaccination is one way to prevent the disease. In addition, though ticks can be found year-round, making sure that you constantly check your dog for ticks during the spring-through-fall peak tick season will help ensure that he does not get the disease. Many people use monthly topical repellents against ticks and fleas on their dogs. As a general rule, these repellants are liquids that are applied to the neck, middle of the back, and base of the back once a month or as indicated by the directions. Alternatively, powders, dips, and other variations are available.

Parainfluenza

Parainfluenza is caused by an extremely contagious virus that can sometimes be fatal in young dogs or those in poor health. This disease is transmitted through upper respiratory secretions. The symptoms of parainfluenza include loss of appetite, discharge from the nose and eyes, sneezing, coughing, difficulty in breathing, and general listlessness. Serious cases may also include pneumonia. The treatment may include antibiotics. In addition, the dog may be placed

The rabies vaccination is mandatory.

on intravenous fluids. The parainfluenza vaccination is given in a series. After that, a booster is typically given annually.

Parvovirus

Parvovirus, prevented by a core vaccination, is a highly contagious and often deadly virus. The symptoms include lethargy, fever, vomiting, and bloody diarrhea. This disease is also transmitted through feces.

Treatment is extensive. Often the veterinarian requires that you hospitalize your puppy for treatment, which may include administering fluids and anti-nausea medication. A puppy or even adult who manages to survive this disease may take many months to recover. In addition, since the disease is so contagious, a surviving

puppy or adult must be kept apart from other dogs for several months.

This vaccination is given in a series, generally starting at six weeks of age. It is then given every three weeks or so until the puppy is four months old. After the initial series is completed, a booster is given on an annual or triennial basis. You'll also need to disinfect with bleach any areas where the infected dog has been. Parvo is so contagious that, in the two cases I know of, the dog and any areas the dog had even walked through were isolated from all other pets. Because of the seriousness of parvovirus, I know of breeders with young puppies who ask that visitors walk through a tray of bleach before coming into their house. Cleaning bedding well and often is also important, as is keeping your yard clean of feces.

Rabies

The rabies vaccination is not only a core vaccination, it is one mandated by all state laws—although some states allow for appropriate titers by your veterinarian after the initial administration of the vaccination. It is usually given to puppies between three and four months of age. Some states require that puppies receive this shot no later than the age of six months. After that, a booster shot is given either every year or every three years depending on the state. Certain universities are now studying the long-term effectiveness of the rabies vaccination to determine how often it can safely be given.

Because this vaccination is mandatory, the vet will issue you a rabies certificate. It is a good idea to carry a copy of this rabies certificate at all times as proof of vaccination. This is especially true if you travel with your dog. If you leave your dog in the care of others while you go on vacation, or if you use a doggy day care center, you may also want to give them a copy. Many training clubs require that you send them a copy to be kept on file at the club.

Rabies is an extremely contagious and deadly disease. Humans can get rabies from the bite or saliva of infected animals. Indeed, dogs can contract rabies from other infected animals, including wild ones. Rabies is still found in this country and certainly is still found abroad.

Spaying and Neutering

Spaying females and neutering males means removing their ability to reproduce. Spaying and neutering are routine surgical procedures performed by veterinarians. In many cases, your puppy will be able to come home the day of or the day after the surgery. Recovery from the surgery is fairly quick, but you will have to keep the puppy quiet and leash-walk him to prevent injuries. After about 14 days, you will need to return to the vet to have the puppy checked and, in cases of external sutures, have them removed.

If you got your puppy from a reliable breeder, she will most likely require that the puppy be spayed or neutered. In fact, this requirement may have even been specified in the contract. In rare cases, a breeder will sell a show-quality puppy and insist that the puppy not be spayed or neutered, because only intact males and females may be shown in the breed ring to their championships. Altered purebred Aussies are still eligible to compete in performance events.

There are, of course, some risks associated with putting any dog under general anesthesia. Most veterinarians are well acquainted with these procedures and perform them often. However, the health and behavior benefits of spaying and neutering far outweigh these risks for the majority of pet owners.

Advantages of Spaying and Neutering

- Spaying and neutering can prevent many forms of cancer. In particular, neutered males are less likely to develop prostate and testicular cancer, and spayed females are less prone to getting mammary and uterine cancer.
- There will be no chance of producing unwanted puppies who could end up in overcrowded shelters or perhaps even euthanized for lack of a good home.
- An unspayed female dog will come into season about every six months. Each season lasts about 23 days. During this time, she must not be around any intact males if you do not want her to become pregnant.
- Unspayed females will disperse drops of blood around the house during her season.
- Many females become very moody and even

downright disagreeable before, during, and after their seasons.

- Some females mistakenly believe that they are pregnant, a condition known as a false pregnancy. They may gather up all their toys, try to nest, and even produce milk. False pregnancies may require veterinary intervention.
- An intact male dog is almost always interested in female dogs—even when the females are not in season.
- Intact male dogs can be more aggressive to handle and manage than neutered males.
- Two intact females are more likely to get into fights than two spayed females; the same is true for two intact males.
- Females cannot compete in obedience, rally, or agility while they are in season. Further, many training clubs will not allow females in heat to train. This means a loss of an average of six weeks of training time a year. Females do not always go into heat when you expect them to go into heat. You could very well enter a show, pay the entry fee, and then find that you are not able to show your female. Given the current cost of entry fees, that can amount to a lot of money.

Females cannot compete in sports while they are in season.

Timing
Accordingly, for most people, the issue is not whether or not they will spay or neuter their puppy; the issue is when is the best time to spay or neuter their puppy. Years ago, the prevailing view was that all puppies (except show puppies) should be spayed or neutered around the age of six months. Most females do not come into season before they are six months old; consequently, the general idea was to spay or neuter puppies before any of them could reproduce.

Today, however, there is a debate about the timing of the spaying and neutering of puppies, and it is a topic you will want to discuss with your veterinarian. Some people believe that even two-month-old puppies can safely be spayed and neutered. Others believe that puppies should be old enough that their growth plates have properly closed before being spayed or neutered. They contend that spaying or neutering before this time will cause the limbs to become overly elongated and too narrow, which makes the dog more susceptible to breaking his limbs.

Should You Breed?
Perhaps you are thinking of not spaying or

neutering because you might want to try your hand at breeding. Keep in mind that it's a tricky business and not for the faint of heart; breeding is an extremely expensive proposition. The initial cost of a show dog is quite high, and most dogs are then shown to their championships before they are bred. Many people use professional handlers in the ring, which can also be quite costly. In addition, there are the actual costs of the shows to take into account.

A good breeder always performs certain genetic tests before a dog is bred. At a minimum, the dog's hips and eyes should be evaluated and cleared. Then add in the average stud fee for a proven dog, which is quite considerable. If your female requires delivery by a cesarean section, that procedure may also

cost quite a lot. Depending on the state of the economy, many a breeder has had extreme difficulties in selling puppies. And providing veterinary care for growing puppies is not inexpensive either.

Further, breeding will take up more of your time than you may realize. Puppies need to be socialized, and a good breeder spends a lot of time socializing a litter. They ask people into their homes to introduce the litter to as many people as possible, which results in a constant flow of guests. After about eight weeks, puppies need to be socialized individually. If not, puppies will bond more to each other than to people. They also need to learn how to sleep separately. And each puppy must be housetrained as well as other initial training. If the litter is not sold at eight weeks, all this

Breeding is an extremely expensive proposition.

If your active Aussie puppy has a sudden change in behavior, go see your vet.

initial training alone will completely consume a breeder's time.

Finding good homes is equally time-consuming. Breeders must conduct extensive interviews of prospective puppy buyers. The breeders ask certain questions, evaluate the candidate, and call the candidate's references. In a similar fashion, the candidates ask the breeders questions and may well ask for references too. This entire process can prove to be stressful for all concerned.

Above all, once a breeder, always a breeder—an ethical breeder will always take back a puppy they bred for the life of the dog. Theoretically, this could become quite a large number of returned adults over time. The returned puppy may not have any manners, and it can be difficult to integrate such a puppy into your home. Worse still, the returned puppy may have an illness and might infect all of your own dogs.

How to Tell if Your Puppy Is Sick

As the saying goes, there is nothing sadder than a sick puppy. And puppies can get very sick very quickly. The best way to prevent this is to be observant—know your puppy. If you see anything out of the ordinary, physically or emotionally, and it lasts for more than a day, take your puppy to the vet. You will never be sorry that you took your puppy to the vet; you may be very sorry if you do not take him often enough.

If you see any change in your puppy's overall condition, he should go to the veterinarian. The coat and skin are important indicators of health. If his coat appears to be sparse or missing patches of hair, or if his skin appears to be dry or red, a veterinarian visit is a good idea. Small bumps anywhere on the skin may indicate problems as well. Anytime a puppy is continuously scratching, he may have a skin issue. Puppies can scratch so much that they cause themselves to bleed. Also, if you notice fleas, you should consult your veterinarian about proper treatment.

If you notice any changes in his bathroom habits, this could be a sign of poor health. If his feces are not the proper consistency or usual color, he may be ill. If he is urinating a lot more or a lot less frequently, or if the amount he is urinating is much greater or much less, he is most likely ill. If you see any straining while the puppy is eliminating, this could also indicate a serious problem.

Australian Shepherd puppies are extremely active—they are constantly racing around. Sometimes they take on more than they bargained for and end up hurting a paw. If your puppy does not put full weight on a paw for over an hour, you should take him to the veterinarian. If your puppy suddenly loses all interest in playing or starts to hold himself differently (e.g., arching his back), he may be ill.

Puppies love to chew, and many love to swallow what they chew—whether or not the item is digestible. If you notice that your puppy has eaten something he shouldn't have, then quickly take him to the vet. Sometimes puppies grab something that gets stuck in their mouth or throat. They may even start drooling copiously. This could be a medical emergency, and you should seek help.

Any time a puppy refuses to eat more than one meal, you need to take him to the vet. There is no such thing as an anorexic Australian Shepherd, puppy or adult.

If you see a runny discharge from the eyes, ears, or nose—especially a yellow or green discharge—it is time to take your puppy to the vet. The same goes for whenever a puppy is constantly shaking his head, as if trying to clear his ears, or if you notice a distinct odor emanating from the puppy's ears.

Excessive and uncontrollable coughing may also indicate that your puppy is sick, as does constant crying. This is especially true for an otherwise normally quiet and content puppy.

On a less subtle note, if your puppy has diarrhea (especially bloody diarrhea), or if your puppy is vomiting (especially bloody vomit), it is a serious matter, and he needs to go to the vet as soon as possible. The same goes if your puppy has trouble breathing. Puppies with internal infections may try to bite their sides and need professional help. If, for any reason, your puppy's gums turn white, rush to an emergency veterinary clinic.

Obviously, if your puppy is involved in a serious accident, you should immediately go to the vet. The same is true if your puppy is involved in a dog fight.

In addition to physical signs of possible illness, you also want to be aware of any emotional signs. Australian Shepherd puppies are almost always very happy and active. It's a bad sign if your puppy suddenly loses interest in the world. Listlessness and lethargy are also danger signs. You need to go see a veterinarian in such cases.

CHAPTER 4

TRAINING YOUR AUSTRALIAN SHEPHERD PUPPY

One of the most enjoyable and rewarding activities for both you and your puppy is training. There are many aspects to training, and one way to help you through it is to find a training club and a trainer. You'll have to socialize your puppy, which is an essential part of training—especially for herding dogs. Puppies need crate training and, of course, housetraining. You should also teach your puppy basic obedience commands, such as *come, down, sit,* and *walk nicely on a leash,* all of which will make him a better house dog.

WHY TRAINING IS IMPORTANT

All puppies need to be trained to learn how to live within a family. A well-trained puppy becomes a well-trained adult, and everyone can agree that well-trained adult dogs are easier to live with and much more likely to become an integral part of the family. And what Australian Shepherds want most is to be a member of the family.

You have probably heard sad stories about puppies who were not adequately trained and became unruly, totally unmanageable adults. Adult Australian Shepherds can weigh at least 40 to 50 pounds (18 to 23 kg), if not more. That is a lot of unmanageable dog to have around the house. It is tragic (terribly sad) when dogs who are not properly trained have to be isolated from the family. Most of these untrained dogs cannot meet any visiting friends and family. Dogs are, after all, pack animals; they need to become part of the family. Do your puppy and yourself a favor—train him! You'll be surprised how much fun you can have together.

Australian Shepherds are especially intelligent and active puppies. And this active nature isn't just satisfied through daily physical outlets. They need mental workouts as well—every day. Training fulfills this mental exercise requirement. In addition, this breed was developed to herd livestock—all Aussies had jobs in the past. Today, even though they might not be herding, they still need a job to do, and training gives them a great job. Most Aussies *love* training time, and all of them *need* training time.

Training is a great way to bond with your puppy and understand his individual nature. You'll discover that your puppy will learn some things easier than others. As with children, each puppy is an individual and has his own preferences, and training him affords you

Australian Shepherds are especially intelligent and active puppies.

Positive Training

Not too long ago, dog training was taught in a negative manner. The modern method of training is to use positive methods. Instead of correcting bad behavior, the trainer rewards good behavior. Rewards can consist of food (treats), toys (playing games), and even just a simple verbal "good job!" Unwanted behavior is never rewarded.

The best trainers try to figure out what motivates a puppy—what makes him more likely to do something. They then use these motivations as rewards. For example, most Australian Shepherd puppies love eating treats, so food is a huge motivator for this breed. Using food as a reward is a great way to get your puppy to do a certain behavior.

Training Keys

One of the most important keys to training your puppy is fairness. It is your responsibility to make sure he understands exactly what you expect of him. There are no shades of gray in dog training, only black and white—you must be very clear with your dog. If your dog is not picking up a command, teach it to him in a way he can understand. Break down the exercise into smaller components, or take out some of the components. Set him up for success by making it easier for him to understand what you want.

Patience is another key to puppy training. Training can be a bit of a yo-yo process. A puppy may appear to understand an exercise, perform it well, and then seem to forget how to do the exercise at all! Learning a new behavior or command takes time for a puppy to process, and it's normal for him to be a bit erratic at first. This is when you must be patient—and fair. Soon enough, your puppy will begin to do the exercise correctly again, and the relearning phase is much shorter than

the opportunity to determine what they are. Extremes in preferences, however, should be discussed with your trainer. Puppies who are overly shy will need additional and more specialized training exercises. On the other hand, puppies who tend to be more dominant will need different, yet equally individualized, training exercises. Some puppies will vacillate between these two extremes; others will stay more or less in the middle range.

Training an Australian Shepherd while he is a puppy is a great way for him to learn exactly what you expect from him. Dogs need to be taught their owner's expectations. While many puppies will test these expectations, they will more readily accept your limitations when they are still puppies than if you start out with an untrained adult. Puppies don't have any ingrained bad habits, and it is up to you to train your puppy to have good ones.

the initial learning phase.

Also, it is critical to end a training session on a positive note. Stop training when your puppy has done a good job—when he has performed what you asked him to do. If he is having trouble with a new command, ask him to execute a command that he already knows well. Once he does that, it is time to stop training for that session.

Last, it is important that you as the trainer have fun while training. Australian Shepherd puppies have an emotional antenna—they know immediately if you are having fun or if you are miserable. If you are really enjoying training, chances are that your puppy will enjoy training right along with you. Even puppies can read human body language exceptionally well. Try to smile and keep your body loose, and you will go a long way toward convincing your puppy that training is great!

FINDING A TRAINER

Ideally, you should try to find a trainer with whom you feel comfortable—much like your relationship with your puppy's veterinarian. You need a good working relationship with both of these professionals in order to help your puppy live a long and happy life.

You can locate a suitable trainer in much the same way that you found your veterinarian. Ask your breeder and your dog-owning friends for recommendations. However, unlike veterinarians, dog trainers are not universally licensed. Therefore, it's all the more important that you find one through good references.

You should then observe a class instructed by the recommended trainer. Do you think you could participate in her class and enjoy being there? Ideally, the training facility should be close to your home. Look around to see if the facility is clean. You will also want to make sure that the puppies in the class appear to be

Multi-Dog Tip

If you have more than one dog, then train them one at a time. When you train your older dog, put your puppy into a nearby crate so that he can watch you train your older dog but cannot interfere with the training.

healthy and that none appear to be aggressive. If you like what you see, at the end of the class, ask the trainer if you can ask her some questions. Asking these questions will give you a chance to ascertain whether or not you could work with this particular trainer.

Questions should include the following:
- Where did you learn to train dogs?
- Do you have any special accreditations?
- What breed and how many dogs do you own?
- Are you familiar with training herding dogs in general and Australian Shepherds in particular?
- How many years have you been teaching?
- How many years have you been teaching at that particular place?
- Do you compete with your own dogs? If so, in what venues?
- How many obedience titles have you earned with your dogs?
- What are the specific obedience titles that you have achieved with your dogs?
- How much does each class cost?
- What times and days are classes given? Are there evening and weekend classes?
- Do you have an assistant to help with the class? If so, what are the assistant's qualifications?

SOCIALIZATION

Socialization is the process of teaching your new puppy about the world. Socialization involves exposing your puppy to new people, places, and noises and generally to the world at large. Remember that the world is entirely new to your puppy—he has never experienced most of the things in it.

All puppies need to be socialized, but is it especially essential for herding dogs, who generally have high energy and high drive. And among the herding breeds, Australian Shepherds definitely must be socialized. Ideally, your breeder has already begun the process of socializing your puppy. Good breeders have safe, interesting objects in the puppy pen as a way to expose puppies to new things. They may have mirrors hanging at a safe distance outside the pen. They make different types of loud noises around the puppies. Most of all, breeders invite friends and family to come play with the puppies from the time that they can see, hear, and walk. By so doing, these breeders are giving their puppies the very best chance at becoming well-adjusted adults.

During a puppy's first few months of life, he will go through various fear periods. This is why socialization is a must-do responsibility from the time you get your puppy through his first year (at the very least). You can never over-socialize a puppy. You can, however, entirely ruin an otherwise good-tempered puppy through lack of socialization. A poorly socialized puppy will never reach his full potential, which is another reason why the importance of proper socialization cannot be overstated.

How to Socialize Your Puppy

The good news is that socializing your puppy is a lot of fun. The idea is to take your puppy to new places and have him meet new people as much as possible. If you work full time, go out during the evenings, and most certainly go out every Saturday and Sunday.

Take your puppy everywhere you can possibly think of to take him. Of course, you will keep your puppy on a leash at all times. Have your puppy walk on different types of surfaces, including grass, linoleum, asphalt, and the like. Some stores allow you to bring puppies inside, which is great way to meet new people, but only do this as long as your puppy has been sufficiently vaccinated as recommended by your veterinarian. You can certainly walk your puppy around the outside of malls in your area. You can even go to ball games and

Treats are a great way to motivate your puppy.

If you socialize your puppy thoroughly, he'll have the best chance of becoming a well-adjusted adult.

sit apart from the crowd of people but let your puppy see and hear all the commotion.

Daily walks are another good way to increase socialization opportunities. The interesting thing about a daily walk, even if it is always around your own block, is that things change every day. One day, the garbage cans may be out on the curb for pickup. The next day, the garbage cans may be back in the yards. Some dogs are very concerned about these slight changes in their world, so getting your puppy used to change will be good for him.

Socialization also includes exposing your new puppy to different types of people. This includes elderly people, children, people of different colors, and people wearing strange attire, such as hats, ties, and raincoats. In all cases, when meeting new people, do not get close enough to

the new people to allow your puppy to get into trouble. The idea is to have the *puppy* approach the people. Never allow anyone to rush toward your puppy and scare him. Meeting new people should be a positive experience, not a scary one. Your puppy kindergarten instructor (which is discussed in the next section), can properly instruct you about how to introduce your puppy to new people.

Your role is to act as if all these new places and people are very interesting, while remaining entirely matter of fact. If you act concerned, your fear will travel down the leash to your puppy. Remember that puppies are our emotional antennae—they follow our lead on how to react, especially in new situations.

Let us say, for example, that while on a walk, your puppy notices an overflowing garbage

Allow your puppy to experience different surfaces.

can on the street for pickup and he reacts to this new image. He may be used to seeing the garbage can empty and by the side of the house and decide that a full garbage can is very scary. He may stop in his tracks. His rear legs may start to shake. What you should do in these situations is act totally unconcerned. Act nonchalant, and tell your puppy what an interesting sight you are seeing. While so doing, reach out and pat the garbage can and put a treat next to it. Just about every puppy will then race up to the garbage can, eat the treat, and forget that the garbage can was ever scary. Treats go a long way in a puppy's mind toward overcoming new, scary situations. For this reason, it is always helpful to carry a supply of treats with you when socializing your puppy.

A word of caution is in order: If, while socializing your puppy to new people and new places, you cannot get your puppy under control, simply walk away. Never allow your puppy to get close enough to someone or something to get into trouble. If you find you can't control your puppy, immediately seek the advice of a behaviorist specializing in helping dogs with socialization problems.

PUPPY KINDERGARTEN

Puppy kindergarten is just about everyone's favorite class! It is your puppy's very first class, which makes it special for both of you. While the structure can vary from class to class, it almost always includes elements of both socialization and obedience training. A typical day at puppy kindergarten consists of some puppy playtime, learning a new basic obedience command, and then learning a new trick.

Some classes begin by allowing puppies to play with each other off leash. This teaches puppies, especially those who are the only dogs in a family, how to play nicely with other dogs. Puppy class also introduces dogs to other breeds. Often puppies are allowed to play with similarly sized puppies. A toy puppy should not play with a giant breed puppy, because there's a good chance the larger puppy could accidentally hurt the smaller one. Australian Shepherd puppies are medium-sized puppies, as are many common household breeds such as Labrador Retrievers, Golden Retrievers, and Standard Poodles.

After the puppies have played and are a bit tired, the obedience part of puppy kindergarten usually begins. Over the course of all the classes, which lasts approximately eight weeks or so, the instructor will show you how to teach your dog basic commands. In all likelihood, the instructor will cover the obedience commands of *come, down, sit,* and *walk nicely on a leash.* The instructor can

be invaluable in showing you how to teach these basic commands before you try them yourself. The instructor can also be helpful in cases where your puppy may have difficulty understanding a command or some part of a command. Many times, the instructor will also explain how to teach your puppy a few tricks. Australian Shepherds are athletic dogs, and most of them enjoy learning tricks.

Some classes also offer introductions to different surfaces and obstacles as socialization exercises. For example, some classes have pieces of artificial turf so that the puppies can walk over this new type of surface. Other classes may have Hula-Hoops on the ground so that the puppies can walk over them. (Jumping through a hoop should not be allowed for puppies, because they are still growing and their joints and bones have not yet completely formed.)

Many puppy kindergarten classes culminate in an actual graduation ceremony. Some even have elaborate graduations, but this depends on the good nature of the instructor and your fellow students. The instructor usually has some sort of diploma to hand to you and almost always also has a very large treat to give

Puppy kindergarten is a great way to socialize your puppy to other dogs.

Many puppy kindergarten classes require that your puppy already has received his first two vaccinations, which usually occurs when he is about nine weeks old. At that point, and in consultation with your veterinarian, try to find a puppy kindergarten class that is about to start. The sooner you begin socializing and training your new puppy, the happier both of you will be in the long run.

to your puppy. You and your classmates can walk individually across the room to receive these honors. Often there is a class picture. If not, you can always invite friends and family to attend and to take pictures for you.

Many graduations include cookies, cakes, and punch for you and your guests. All in all, puppy kindergarten, and most especially puppy kindergarten graduation, is a fun time for everyone. Even the puppies seem to get a big kick out of it.

How to Find the Right Class for Your Puppy

The best way to find a good puppy kindergarten class is to ask around. Start by asking your veterinarian if she has any recommendations. If you have already found a training club through her help, the club president will be able to direct you to the appropriate class. However, many training clubs have puppy kindergarten class only when they have enough puppies interested in attending, so often this is not a class offered

continuously. For this reason, it is good to make these inquiries even before you bring your puppy home. You can then be put on a waiting list for the next available puppy kindergarten class.

CRATE TRAINING

Simply put, crate training is the process of acclimating your puppy to accept and even enjoy spending time in a crate. The idea behind crate training is based on the nature of dogs. Dogs are den animals. In the wild, they prefer to sleep in dens—probably for safety reasons. Done correctly, crate training is simply an extension of a dog's natural behavior in the wild. However, crate usage can be abused. No dog should remain crated all day and all night. The crate should be an enjoyable place, not a prison. Along the same lines, a crate should never be used for punishment.

Crate training is a necessary precursor to housetraining your puppy. Moreover, puppies don't have good "house sense." Left unattended, they can destroy a house rather quickly and, even worse, can easily seriously injure or kill themselves. It is guaranteed that a puppy left by himself in the house for too long will get into serious trouble. Crate training provides a safe alternative to all this potential destruction and injury.

After you successfully crate train your puppy, you should never have to retrain him to accept a crate. The younger your puppy, the easier it will be for him to accept crate training.

How to Crate Train Your Puppy

You should already have a crate in place before you bring your puppy home. A properly sized crate gives the puppy enough room to stand up and turn around comfortably. If you give a puppy too much room in a crate, he will tend to soil one end. And, as I mentioned in

Chapter 2, you've hopefully had a huge jumpstart on crate training by asking your breeder to put your puppy in a crate a day or two before you pick him up. If you followed through with this advice, you will be very thankful you did.

Most people keep crates in their bedroom. This way, the puppy can still see, hear, and smell you. Dogs are pack animals and need the comfort of the pack. Even though he may be unhappy about being in a crate at first, he will be comforted by being in the same room with you.

The first step is to introduce the crate to your puppy as a safe place. After he settles in on his first day with you, show him the crate. Keep the crate door open. In fact, even when the crate is not in use, it is a good idea to keep the crate door open. You want your puppy to be attracted enough to the crate—his special den—that he feels fine going in and out of it while you are there to supervise him.

You may want to feed him his first meal in his crate. You can also give him a few treats in the crate now and then during the first day. He will begin to associate the crate with food, which is a positive, high motivator for puppies.

The next step is to give him a safe toy, like the ones Nylabone makes, that he can play with only while in the crate. Then say something along the lines of "crate time," and toss a very special treat into the back of the crate. Your puppy will likely go inside to eat the treat. While he is busy eating in the back of the crate, quickly close the door. Note that some crates have one latch and others have two. For puppies, two latches are better, because if by any chance you forget to close one, then the

Want to Know More?

To learn more about which crate is right for your puppy, go to Chapter 2: Finding and Prepping for Your Australian Shepherd Puppy.

other is still closed. Always check and double check to make sure that the latches are closed.

The first night your puppy spends in his crate can be difficult for both of you. Many puppies cry a lot when they realize that they are physically constrained in a crate. Most of these puppies will settle down and go to sleep in due time. Your role that first night is to be strong. You should not open the door and let the puppy out when he cries this first night. If you do, then you will teach your puppy that whenever he cries, you will let him out of his crate.

The second night and the rest of the week should be easier. Your puppy should cry less and less each night. By the end of the week (if not sooner), he should go into his crate quickly and easily and should not cry.

Some puppies wake up in the middle of the night and cry. If this happens, it likely that your puppy has to go to the bathroom. Open the crate door and immediately put a collar and leash on your puppy. Then walk him outside to do his business. When completed, walk him back to his crate, remove the collar and leash, toss another treat into the back of the crate, close and latch the door, and then both of you should be able to sleep through the rest of the night. Once your puppy has a reliable *come* command, he will no longer need to be leashed before going out, but by then, he will probably be able to sleep through the night as well.

By the same token, if your puppy wakes up early in the morning and starts to cry, he probably has to go to the bathroom again. Puppies do not know the difference between a weekday morning and a weekend morning. Their schedule tends to follow the weekdays, so he will probably wake up at the same time every morning, including on weekends. As he matures, he will allow you to sleep in. For now, however, when he cries in the morning, you must take him outside to relieve himself.

HOUSETRAINING

Housetraining is one of the most important lessons you will teach your new puppy. Simply put, housetraining is the process of training your Australian Shepherd puppy to eliminate outside (not inside) your home. Not too long ago, the idea of housetraining struck fear in the hearts of many new pet owners. Today, however, housetraining is readily accomplished by most pet owners. Setting up a schedule and crate training greatly facilitate the process of housetraining, which requires consistency on your part.

Some breeders now litter box train their puppies starting at around three weeks of age, which is when puppies first walk. By the time these puppies are eight weeks old, they are basically housetrained. If you buy your puppy from a breeder who has already done the preliminary work of housetraining him, your job will be much easier.

How to Housetrain

Puppies have extremely small bladders, especially when they are only eight or nine weeks old, so they have very little bladder

Crate training is a necessary precursor to housetraining your puppy.

control. Australian Shepherd puppies are very clean and want to stay that way, but at that young age, they may not realize *when* they are about to eliminate. This is especially true for urination. The surest way to avoid accidents is for you to take the puppy outside often (every 15 minutes) and at the times described below while he is young. As he matures, you can extend the time between bathroom breaks.

Generally speaking, puppies develop control over when they need to defecate before they obtain control over when they need to urinate. In some cases, males can take a little longer to develop bathroom control than females. However, Australian Shepherd puppies truly dislike soiling their crate. It is your responsibility to take the puppy outside enough so that he does not have to eliminate in his crate.

You can also train your puppy to potty on command. Use a phrase such as *do your business*. Each time you take your puppy outside, say "do your business," and after he eliminates, say "good do your business," and act like a miracle happened. Throw a party!

You do not need to take him to the same spot outside every time; however, you should always take your puppy out the same door to go to the bathroom. In due time, he will learn to "ask" to go outside by going to that same door and perhaps even making a noise. At this point, if you prefer not to hear him cry to go outside, then you can put sleigh bells on the door handle. Every time your puppy asks to go outside, ring the bells and say "outside." Eventually your brilliant puppy will learn to ring the bells to go outside.

Stick to a Schedule

If you take your puppy outside to potty at the following times, he will be housetrained very quickly:

You can train your Aussie to potty on command.

- When he first wakes up—this includes if he wakes up during the night.
- After he finishes eating and again about 15 minutes later.
- At eight or nine weeks of age, every 15 minutes while awake; this time interval increases as the puppy ages.
- After playing or other strenuous activity.
- If you notice that he has passed gas.
- Right before bedtime.
- In the middle of the night if he starts to cry.
- Anytime he starts circling, which most dogs do as a prelude to going to the bathroom.
- Whenever he asks to go outside.
- Anytime you even *think* that he *may* be asking to go outside.

Changes in your puppy's bathroom habits may be a sign of illness.

Health Check

Be aware of any changes in your puppy's bathroom habits, since it could be a sign of illness that must be addressed by your veterinarian. If your puppy suddenly starts to urinate in much bigger or much smaller amounts, or with greater or lesser frequency, there could be a problem. Diarrhea or constipation is also a sign of problems. An outright danger sign is the presence of blood in either the urine or feces. Along the same lines, changes in the color or smell of either the urine or the feces are danger signs.

Dealing With Accidents

There are two special supplies (other than the crate) you will need for housetraining. First, you will need a lot of paper towels. Second, you will need a good product for removing accidents, preferably a product with active enzymes that break down the urine.

When—not if—your puppy has an accident, do not make a fuss. He does not understand the concept of being housetrained, so it is not fair to yell at him. Also, he has a tiny bladder and very little control. Plus, if you had watched your puppy closely enough and adhered to the schedule, he would not have had the accident. After you clean up the accident using the enzymatic cleaner, take your puppy outside. Be consistent and stick to the schedule, and one day, you will wake up and realize that your Aussie is indeed housetrained. It is almost that simple.

Submissive Urination

Some puppies develop submissive urination, which should not be confused with a housetraining accident. They get so overwhelmingly happy to see new visitors or even to see you that they accidentally release a small amount of urine. Try to be very calm when this occurs, and consult your veterinarian about the problem.

BASIC OBEDIENCE COMMANDS

There are a few basic obedience commands that will make integrating your Australian Shepherd puppy into your family unit a lot easier. A little obedience every day in short (ten-minute or so) sessions will also provide mental exercise for your puppy. You'll be giving him the job of learning early obedience commands, which will be in keeping with his needs as a herding dog bred to work. Keep in mind, however, that puppies have extremely short attention spans. Ten minutes a day for a young puppy is more than enough. You do not want to overly tire or bore him when you are training—you want him to love being trained. Above all, training has to be fun for smart puppies like Aussies. It is up to you, as the trainer, to make training fun for your puppy.

The first step is to teach a *release* command, which tells your puppy that he has done exactly what you asked him to do and is now free to do as he wants. After that, you can teach the basic obedience commands *come when called*, *down*, *sit*, and *walk nicely on a leash*.

Initially, you should introduce all new concepts in your own home or back yard. Make sure the environment is quiet and safe. You do not need any distractions at this point. At the end of your training session, you can offer your puppy a toy as an extra bonus and relax while you watch him play. Nylabone makes several toys specially designed for puppies.

When it comes to training treats, whatever you use should be used only as treats and not for general food. String cheese is a great natural and healthy training treat. Different treats have different values to individual dogs, so you will learn which treats your dog values most and use only the highest valued treats when necessary as, for example, when learning new behaviors. If you feed bedtime treats, they should not be the same treats you use for training.

Release

Every puppy should understand when he is no longer being trained and that he is free to continue playing or doing whatever he feels like doing. This is known as a *release* command. Many people use the word *free* as the *release* command.

It is important to always treat your dog after he executes a command properly and before releasing him. In time, with older puppies, you can combine a series of commands and releases. For example, ask the puppy to do one command, reward him, release him, and then ask him to do another command.

Come When Called

Learning to come when called is absolutely necessary for every single puppy. In some cases,

Training Tidbit

Teach your puppy to look at you when you want his attention. When he is near you, say his name followed by a word such as *look*. When he looks at you, immediately say "good look," give him a treat, and release him. You can then use this command whenever you want him to look at you, such as before teaching other commands.

When teaching the *come* command, you can slowly increase the length of the leash.

the *come when called* command could save your puppy's life. For example, your puppy could suddenly get loose from your back yard or house and run toward a car. If he knows to come when called each and every time, your puppy will remain safe.

The easiest way to teach a puppy to come when called is:

- Put your puppy on a 6-foot (2-m) leash, and make sure you have treats in your pocket.
- Wait until your puppy is looking directly at you.
- At that precise moment, call him to you in an encouraging voice; most people use the puppy's name followed by the word *come*.
- At the same time, hold the treat close to his eye level and wave it around so that he is sure to see it.
- When he comes to you, and he will, very enthusiastically say "good come," and at the same time, give him a treat.
- Then release him.
- You should act very, very happy and make an enormous fuss over his brilliance in coming when called.

Over time, your puppy will become more reliable and faster with this command. You can then slowly increase the length of the leash. You can purchase leashes in various lengths at most pet stores.

It's important to note that you should ask your puppy to come when called only for a positive experience. In other words, never ask your puppy to come and then do something he views as unpleasant. You want your puppy to think that every time you call him and he comes to you, he will be rewarded. To be even more positive, you can give him a treat every single time he comes when called for his entire first year. You may even want to use a special treat that you pull out only for coming when called.

Sit

The *sit* command involves teaching your puppy to sit on his behind with his front feet in front of him. There are many uses for the *sit*. Many people ask their adult dogs to sit before they are given their meals or before they put on their dog's leash. Some ask that their dogs sit again before they go out of the house together. If you meet a friend during a walk, you may ask your dog to sit while you talk with your friend.

Unless you plan on doing formal obedience, you do not really need to be concerned about whether your puppy sits by drawing his hind legs forward toward his front legs or his front legs back toward his hind legs. All you really want is to get your puppy to sit.

To teach *sit*:
- Put your puppy on a 6-foot (2-m) leash.
- Put some nice treats into your pocket, but keep one out in your right hand.
- Hold the leash in your left hand.
- When your puppy is looking at you, say his name followed by the word *sit*.
- At the same time, slowly move the treat above his head.
- As you move the treat above his head, also move it backward toward his body and then down a little bit lower—but no lower than

Unless you intend to compete in formal obedience, it doesn't matter how your puppy lies down.

the top of his neck. Do not move the treat any further or lower than this.

- For the puppy to eat the treat, he has to lower his head and then move his head a little backward. His body follows his head, and he ends up in a *sit* position.
- Immediately when your puppy sits, say "good sit," and offer him the treat.
- You can reinforce the *sit* position by giving the puppy his treat at mouth level.
- Of course, you should also act very enthusiastic about his *sit*, praising him for doing a good job.

At first, ask your puppy to stay in a *sit* for only a split second.

- Then release.

After your puppy understands the *sit* command, slowly increase the length of time you ask the puppy to remain in a *sit* position. At this stage, you should ask him to stay in a *sit* for only a split second—that is practically an eternity for a young puppy.

Down

The *down* command teaches a puppy to lie down. You can use this command in your everyday lives. Some people ask their older dogs to down while they are eating their meals at the table. It is also useful to have your older dog lie down when you are grooming him. In an emergency, if your puppy gets out of your yard or home, you can control him at a distance by telling him to down and then take him back home.

Unless you intend to compete in formal obedience, it does not really matter how the puppy lies down, whether he uses his front legs first or his rear legs first, or in what position he lies down on the floor. Some puppies lie in strict positions like a Sphinx, with their elbows touching the floor and their rear legs under them. Other puppies choose to have their elbows on the floor and then shift over on one hip. Some actually lie flat on the floor.

To teach the *down*:

- Put your puppy on a 6-foot (2-m) leash.
- Find some nice treats and put them into your pocket, but keep one in your hand.
- Put your leash into your left hand and a treat into your right hand at his eye level.
- Make sure that your puppy is looking at you, then say his name followed by the word *down*.
- At the same time, slowly lower the treat to the ground.
- As you lower the treat to the ground, also move the treat toward the puppy so that his head moves toward his body.

- For the puppy to eat the treat, he has to lower his head; his body follows his head, and he ends up in the *down* position.
- As soon as the puppy lies down, say "good down," and then give him the treat.
- To reinforce the *down* position, give the puppy his treat at floor level and under his head.
- As with any exercise, act extremely happy and praise his performance.
- Then, as with any exercise, release.

Over time, you can increase the length of time you ask the puppy to remain in the *down* position. For the moment, however, you should not ask him to stay down for more than a second. Puppies have too much energy to stay down for much longer than that.

Walk Nicely on a Leash

Since daily walks are a critical part of socializing your new puppy, it is imperative that you teach him to walk nicely on a leash. You do not want to end up with a 50-pound (23-kg) adult dog pulling you down the road or knocking you over. The time to teach your puppy to walk without pulling is now—when you first begin your walks together. Walks are themselves strong motivators and, eventually, your daily walks can motivate your dog to walk nicely on his leash.

Initially, however, you have to teach your puppy how to walk nicely together with you

Leash Width

Australian Shepherd puppies grow quickly. Ask your vet or trainer about the correct width for your leash. Wider leashes have heavier metal snaps, which may be too much weight for your puppy. The first time you teach your puppy to accept a leash, make sure that the snap is not too heavy.

on a leash. To start, you must introduce your puppy to the idea of a leash as a means of walking together. You can start in your home or secure back yard. Put the collar on your puppy with the leash already attached. Then walk around a little while you let the puppy drag the leash, but be very careful not to accidentally step on it.

Once the puppy is used to dragging the leash, you can then pick up the other end. Start by talking to him so that you keep his attention. Take a step, and when he follows along with you, give him a treat. You need to let your puppy know that being next to you involves getting lots of good treats! When he is able to walk with you like this in your home and back yard, you are ready to go outside and begin your walks together. Remember to bring a lot of treats for your daily walks, and reward him when he's walking nicely.

PART II

ADULTHOOD

CHAPTER 5

FINDING YOUR AUSTRALIAN SHEPHERD ADULT

Instead of getting a puppy, many people prefer to get an adult Australian Shepherd. When is an Aussie considered an adult? Australian Shepherds physically mature at around two years of age, but many do not fully mentally mature until they are three years old.

Several options are available for those who decide to find an adult, including rescue organizations, animal shelters, and breeders.

WHY GET AN ADULT?

A great benefit of adopting an adult dog is that he will not need the same amount of time and attention that a puppy needs. The time and energy necessary to properly raise an Australian Shepherd puppy from the age of eight weeks onward should not be underestimated. Raising puppies is hard work; raising active and athletic Aussie puppies can be extremely hard work. Many adults available for adoption are already housetrained and crate trained, and they may even know some basic obedience. If you are lucky, they will also have been well socialized. In short, adopting an adult Australian Shepherd may be a great shortcut to a nice family pet.

Aside from making life a bit easier, the main reason many people adopt or rescue an adult is that by so doing, they save a dog's life. It can be a true source of pride to adopt an adult Aussie and save his life.

Disadvantages

There may be certain disadvantages to adopting or rescuing an adult. When you get a puppy from a good breeder, you will know more about what to expect as your puppy ages. The parents have had the necessary health checks, which is not a guarantee but certainly increases the likelihood that your puppy will also be free of certain types of health issues. You can see the parents and littermates yourself. And you will have access to the breeder's vast knowledge and experience, which can be a tremendous benefit.

When you adopt or rescue an adult, you often have no idea about the dog's genetics. You may not know what the dog has been trained or not trained to do. You will need to learn if the dog has developed any bad habits, such as chasing cars or children, jumping backyard fences, or destructive chewing in the house. In short, you probably won't know much about an adopted or rescued dog. However, representatives from adoption organizations, either rescue groups or animal hair in it. Plus, their coat requires weekly grooming. Some owners simply may not be able to provide the care that is needed to own an Australian Shepherd.

In some cases dog owners, through life's misfortunes, have had to turn their dogs into shelters and rescues. In today's economy, some people simply can no longer afford to keep their dogs. Natural disasters often give people no choice but to rehome their dogs because they do not even have homes themselves. Everyone knows about the thousands of dogs and cats who lost their homes in the aftermath of the hurricane Katrina disaster. The Gulf oil spill is another example where a disaster resulted in the displacement of thousands of dogs and cats. Sometimes owners develop heath issues and can no longer care for their dogs. In other words, sometimes the people who turn their dogs in to be adopted are doing so because they simply have no other choice; they are not necessarily bad people, only people with vast misfortune.

ADOPTION OPTIONS

The most common places to find dogs to adopt are either rescue organizations or animal shelters. In addition, breeders may have adults available on occasion.

shelters, do their best to know their dogs and to screen both the dogs and the potential owners for compatibility. Their goal is for the dog and you to be happy together.

Why Dogs End Up in Shelters

Adult dogs are given up for many reasons. Although some dogs available for adoption may have physical or behavioral problems, others are wonderful dogs who were just with the wrong owners. The owner may not have done enough research on the breed, and the dog was simply not a good match with that particular person.

Especially regarding Australian Shepherds, some owners simply may not have been able to provide the care that is needed to own this breed. Australian Shepherds are very active and require a lot of physical and mental exercise. They need to be integrated into the family unit; they do not do well when left alone. Further, there is the hair factor. Australian Shepherds are a coated breed, which means that they generally lose their coats two times a year. Even when they are not blowing coat, any home with an Australian Shepherd has

Rescue Organizations

Rescue organizations are places where people who can no longer care for their dogs (usually a specific breed) voluntarily turn them in for rehoming. The Australian Shepherd Club of America (ASCA) has an official rescue organization called the Aussie Rescue and Placement Helpline, Inc. (ARPH). You can find out more about ARPH at www.aussierescue.org. Plus, there are many other Australian Shepherd rescue organizations throughout the country. Aussie breeders are a good resource for finding

Many rescue organizations carefully screen potential owners to make the best possible match for their dogs and to weed out people whose lifestyles are simply not suitable to this breed.

some of these organizations.

Most rescues are not-for-profit organizations operated by volunteers. They are able to exist through generous donations, including money from people who have adopted their dogs. In some cases, such donations are even tax deductible (which is a matter to discuss with your accountant).

Adoption organizations with available dogs will often post pictures of them on a website, usually by geographical location. If you find a rescue you are interested in, you will probably be asked to complete an application form that will be read and reviewed by a rescue representative. Rescue organizations carefully screen potential owners to make the best possible match for their dogs and to weed

out people whose lifestyles are simply not suitable to this breed. You will be asked many questions to see if you have a suitable home for an Australian Shepherd and, if so, which

Training Tidbit

Remember to ask the adoption organization's staff what, if any, training the dog has been given. Also ask if the dog is able to be in a crate overnight. A crate-trained adult dog will make your life much easier.

- Do you have a fenced yard and, if so, how high is it?
- Do you have children and, if so, what are their ages?
- Do you work full time? How many hours a week?
- Do keep a regular schedule?
- If you work a lot of hours, are you willing to hire a dog walker?
- Have ever trained a dog before and, if so, what did you train the dog to do?
- Are you willing to attend a basic obedience class?
- Are you willing to spay or neuter?

If you have or have had pets, you will be asked for the name of your veterinarian to serve as a reference. Even if you have never had any pets, you will be asked to provide several references. As with most breeders, many rescue organizations also mandate that if, for any reason, you become unable to keep the dog, you must return him to that organization.

particular rescue dog would best fit into your lifestyle.

A typical application or interview will ask the following:

- Why do you want an Australian Shepherd?
- Have you done research about the breed?
- Do you understand, and are you ready to make, the time commitment this breed requires?
- Have you ever owned a dog?
- What breeds have you owned?
- How many dogs do you currently own, and what breed are they?
- Do you have any other animals, such as cats?
- Do you rent or own your home?
- Are there any restrictions on the number of dogs or the size of the dogs you may have? (Even if you own your home, your community may have dog-related covenants or limitations. Some communities limit the number of dogs a person may own, and others even limit the height of a fence or even the ability to put up a fence. Condominium associations may also impose weight restrictions on a dog.)
- If you rent, are there any restrictions your landlord will impose?

The rescue's representatives will also screen their dogs. They generally have a veterinarian evaluate the dog physically to rule out any health issues. The best organizations will also test the dog to assess his overall behavior. For example, they will test if he is able to behave around cats, other dogs, and children. They will determine if he knows basic obedience commands. They will also find out if he is housetrained or crate trained.

When the representative finds the right rescue dog for you, she will arrange for you to meet the dog. The representative may also visit you in your home to make sure that it is right for the dog. If all goes well, then you will complete some adoption paperwork. Since the majority of adoption organizations depend on donations, you may also be asked to make a donation. If you have any questions after you return home with your rescue dog, you can always call the rescue representative for help and advice.

Animal Shelters

Almost every community has a local animal shelter for pets either found as strays or voluntarily given up to the animal shelter. Strays must stay a certain period of time in the shelter before they can be made available for adoption.

The adoption process for animal shelters is similar to that of rescue organizations. You can expect to be screened to determine your suitability for owning a dog, including filling out an application similar to the one discussed for a rescue organization. In many cases, you also will have to pay an adoption fee. The amount of the adoption fee may go up as the size of the dog increases. A 50-pound (23-kg) Australian Shepherd may cost more than a 10-pound (6-kg) Toy Poodle.

Often, animal shelters hold events in local pet stores, where they bring their available dogs and cats. You can then spend some time getting to know the dog you are interested in adopting.

The difference between a shelter and rescue like ARPH is that rescues are exclusively dedicated to rescuing a particular breed—in this case, Australian Shepherds. Rescue organizations are extremely familiar with the characteristics and quirks of their breed. Animal shelters not only take in many different breeds of dogs, they take in all kinds of other sorts of animals, such as cats. Also, animal shelters may or may not know their dogs as well as the rescue organizations know theirs.

On the plus side, certain animal shelters receive financial support directly from their communities. As a result, they may be able to offer follow-up services and benefits that some rescue organizations may not be able to

Some animal shelters hold adoption events in local pet stores.

One of the lesser-known options for finding a nice adult involves Australian Shepherd breeders.

provide. For example, some animal shelters have training classes specifically for their adoptees. Other shelters have fun adoption events that can include having your new dog's photograph taken with you. Many have social events and formal fundraisers that you and your dog can also attend. You can even expand your social network to include others who have adopted dogs from the animal shelter and make some new dog-owning friends. Another positive is that many animal shelters offer continuing medical care at a reduced rate for their dogs, especially reduced-rate rabies vaccinations and spaying and neutering.

Try Volunteering

If you decide to adopt an Australian Shepherd through a rescue organization or from a local animal shelter, you can give something back by becoming a volunteer. These groups are desperately in need of help and would greatly appreciate monetary donations or, better yet, a bit of your time. By so doing, you will also be helping them save homeless animals.

Breeders

One of the lesser-known adoption options involves Australian Shepherd breeders. Many breeders formally evaluate their show prospects at the age of about one year. At that time, they determine whether or not, based on their own lines, this particular one-year-old is likely to develop into a nice dog for the conformation ring and later for breeding purposes.

If a breeder decides that her one-year-old is not going to become her next great show dog,

Want to Know More?

Some people find that the most rewarding dogs of all to adopt are the senior dogs. These dogs do not have the typical problems of puppies. They most likely will not chew their way through your house. They have a much lower energy level and do not need nearly as much physical exercise as do puppies. There is often a special something that you find only in a senior dog's eyes. To learn more about adopting a senior, see Chapter 12: Finding Your Australian Shepherd Senior.

she may decide to offer the dog for private adoption. This does not mean that anything is wrong with the dog. Often the reasons that breeders do not want to use a particular dog in their breeding program are more complicated than the average pet owner even wants to hear. These adult dogs from breeders are typically very nice dogs.

In these cases, the breeder may post the dog on her website announcing that he is now available. The advantage of getting a one-year-old dog from a breeder is that you know exactly where the dog came from and therefore know his parents as well as his genetic background. Further, the breeder will always be available to you as an expert on Australian Shepherds in general and that one dog in particular.

Breeders do not often make their young dogs available, so you may have to wait awhile. The cost may be slightly more than that for dogs adopted from a rescue or a shelter.

CHAPTER 6

AUSTRALIAN SHEPHERD GROOMING NEEDS

Australian Shepherds carry a medium coat with a ruff around the neck, feathers on the legs, and britches on their rears. They are a double-coated breed with both a long outer topcoat and a shorter, denser, and fluffier undercoat. They shed—usually twice a year. The males carry more coat—and it's usually thicker—than do the females. As a result of their coat type, Australian Shepherds require weekly grooming sessions to keep their coats healthy and looking good. A well-groomed Australian Shepherd is indeed a beautiful dog.

Grooming requires brushing, bathing, ear care, eye care, nail trimming, and dental care. You should know how to do all these things for your Australian Shepherd. However, if you decide that grooming your dog is too much for you, you can always use a professional groomer.

Done correctly, your weekly grooming sessions can be quality time spent with your dog. It is also a good opportunity for you to physically check over your dog for any health issues. In addition, you can view grooming as a learning exercise for your dog. Use treats generously to encourage him to allow you to groom him and touch him all over.

BRUSHING

Brushing helps you to maintain your Australian Shepherd's health. His fluffy undercoat can become matted. If left unchecked, mats can cause the skin to develop painful hot spots, which will mean a trip to the veterinarian. Brushing also helps keep the coat clean, as the brush removes superficial dirt. Plus, the oil glands found in a dog's skin help to add shine to the coat when brushed. Brushing is a good time to examine your Aussie's skin to make sure it is a healthy pink color, which is a sign of good health, and does not have any lumps or bumps. At the same time, you can make sure that your dog does not have any fleas or ticks.

Training Tidbit

Grooming can be difficult for a dog at first. To help him make a more positive association with being groomed, give him a super-special treat. Give him these super-special treats only when you are grooming him.

A pin brush works well for brushing your Aussie.

It is especially critical to brush your dog *daily* when he is shedding, which happens about twice a year. An Australian Shepherd will shed his fluffy undercoat, not the topcoat. When an Aussie is about to shed, his hair may appear to be a bit drier and then start to develop clumps close to his skin. All of a sudden, these clumps will be flying all over your house. You will be astounded at the amount of undercoat one dog can shed over the course of three or so weeks—you'll fill up several garbage bags. Even with brushing to help reduce some of the hair that ends up inside your home, you will still use up several vacuum cleaner bags. Don't forget—during shedding time, you will want to brush your dog on a daily basis.

How to Brush

Over time, you will develop a way of brushing that works best for your dog. Here are a few pointers for how to brush your Aussie:

- **Location:** Decide where you will brush your dog. Some people use their living room. You might also want to use a grooming table. Australian Shepherds fit on a medium-sized grooming table. If you use a grooming table, double-check that the legs are properly locked when you set it up.
- **Equipment:** A pin brush of medium pin length works well. In addition, you will need a comb with medium-length pins and a slicker brush. You'll also need medium-sized thinning shears. It's a good idea to keep some treats handy, and it is easier if you have all these tools, including the treats, within easy reach.
- **Inspect:** Take a look at your dog's coat. Make sure that your Aussie does not have any mats in his hair. Overall, your dog's coat should look shiny. He should not be missing any hair, and his skin should be nice and pink. You should not see any areas of red, inflamed skin. If you notice any inflammation, talk to your vet.
- **Line Brushing the Body:** Line brushing basically means brushing the coat outwards and in the direction that the hair grows in long lines. Make short strokes upward using the pin brush. Start by brushing the top of his back, or topline, and then do each side.
- **Brushing the Leg Feathers and Britches:** You should never line brush the feathers on the legs or the britches on the dog's rear. If you do, you will pull out too much of the coat. For these areas, using the pin brush, very gently and slowly brush outward and in the direction the hair is growing. You can then comb these areas—but only very gently.
- **Combing the Head and Face:** Use the comb for the short hair on the head. Gently comb the hair on the head and face. As always, you will comb outward and in the direction the hair is growing.

- **Trimming:** Australian Shepherds are not a sculpted breed, meaning that scissors and grooming shears are not used to excess. The majority of Australian Shepherds are simply tidied up a bit so that there are no loose hairs. The areas that are tidied up are the outside of the ears and the tail. For the ears, gently use the thinning shears to remove any hair beyond the outside of the edge of the ear. For the tail, make a straight line at the base and straight cut across.
- **Treats:** Each time you complete one of the above steps, you may want to reward your dog and give him a treat. If he has a hard time with a particular step, offer him additional treats.

BATHING

A correct Australian Shepherd coat will shed most of the dirt when dry. However, you may still need to give your dog a bath about once a month. If you live in an area with red clay dirt, you may have to bathe him more often. It is also a good idea to bathe your dog after he finishes shedding.

Like brushing, bathing helps to maintain your dog's health and is a good time to check to make sure his skin is a good color. You can also see if he has any other issues, such as lumps, bumps, fleas, or ticks.

Choosing a Shampoo and Conditioner

There are a tremendous variety of shampoos and conditioners available. Be sure to pick ones formulated for a dog, not for people, so that you do not irritate your dog's sensitive skin. Many dogs dislike strongly scented shampoos and conditioners. There are extra-moisturizing shampoos and conditioners that are useful in adding additional moisture after your dog has finished blowing his coat. Some people like to use specially formulated shampoos to enhance any white on the dog. If your dog appears to be itching a lot, which happens before they shed, you may want to choose an oatmeal-based shampoo to soothe his skin. The choice of shampoo and conditioner is, in the end, a personal one and can vary with the condition of your dog.

How to Bathe

- **Location:** The easiest place to bathe your dog is in your bathtub. You will need a hand-held shower attachment and a screen to fit over the drain. The screen will trap hair that falls out and save you a visit from your plumber. Last, you will need two thick rubber mats to put down in the tub. The mats will prevent your dog from sliding and getting scared.
- **Equipment:** You'll need shampoo, conditioner, towel, blow dryer (optional), and treats. Never leave your dog unattended in the tub, so before you get started, put the shampoo and conditioner by the tub. If you bought a large size of shampoo and conditioner, you can also put some into smaller containers that are easy to hold and squeeze with one hand.

By the Numbers

Bathing an Australian Shepherd should take less than half an hour and usually does not need to be done more than once a month. The weekly grooming sessions should not take more than a half an hour.

2. Never put anything down into the ear canal—your goal is to clean only the inner surface of the ear flap.

How to Care for Your Dog's Ears

- **Location:** You will want to care for your dog's ears in the same general area as you do your overall grooming.
- **Equipment:** You first need to obtain an ear-cleaning product from your veterinarian or pet store. You will also need cotton balls. Have your thinning shears nearby as well as some treats.
- **Inspect:** If you notice any foul smell or discoloration, or if your dog continuously shakes his head vigorously from side to side, you should take him to your veterinarian. These can be signs of an ear infection.
- **Apply Cleaning Product:** Read all the instructions first. Then put some cleaning product on a cotton ball. Gently rub the inner surface of each ear flap with the cotton ball.
- **Trim Hair Around Ears:** Using the thinning shears, gently trim the hair around the outside edge of the ear.
- **Treats:** When you have finished taking care of your Aussie's ears, tell him he is a good dog, and give him a treat.

Some people find it easier to use a grooming table for their Aussie.

EYE CARE

Some breeds of dogs have certain eye issues requiring a lot of care. Fortunately, Australian Shepherds do not need more than minimal care of their eyes.

How to Care for Your Dog's Eyes

- **Location:** As with ear care, you can care for your dog's eyes in the same area in which you do most of your other grooming.
- **Equipment:** You will need only a cotton ball for general eye care.
- **Inspect:** Take a good look at your dog's eyes. Although dogs may have a little sand or mucus in the corner of their eyes, you should never see either one in excessive amounts. Your dog's eyes should never be continuously tearing either. In particular, thick or yellow mucus can be indicative of an eye infection. If you see your dog blinking constantly and rapidly and perhaps even pawing at his eyes, he may have something in his eye. In such cases, take him to your veterinarian.
- **Gently Wipe Eyes:** Put a small amount of lukewarm water onto the cotton ball. Then, very gently, wipe away any mucus or

sand from the corner of your dog's eyes. Of course, you must be mindful not to accidentally touch the eye with the cotton ball.

- **Treats:** Upon completion of caring for your dog's eyes, let him know he is a good dog by giving him a treat.

NAIL TRIMMING

It is especially important to trim your dog's nails on a weekly basis. If a dog's nails grow too long, it becomes uncomfortable for him to walk, much less run. In addition, overly long nails cause the dog to rock back on his legs, which, in turn, can damage the lower leg.

At first, many dogs do not like having their nails trimmed. If you begin early, when your Aussie is a young puppy, and take your time about the whole process, then he'll soon learn to accept having his nails trimmed. If you simply cannot trim your dog's nails, then you need to have a professional groomer take care of them. Either way, you must make sure that your dog's nails are properly trimmed once a week without fail.

There are two methods of trimming a dog's nails. The first, which will be discussed here, involves using a nail clipper. The second method involves the use of a grinding tool. If you decide that you want to grind the nails, you should first ask a professional groomer how to do it. (How to find a professional groomer will be discussed at the end of this chapter.) If necessary, you can pay the professional groomer to teach you how to grind your dog's nails. For most people, however, the nail clipper is the easiest way of maintaining their dog's nails.

How to Trim Your Dog's Nails

- **Exercise Your Dog:** Many dogs accept grooming as part of their lives without

objection, but more than a few do not enjoy having their nails trimmed. Before trimming your dog's nails, you should first thoroughly exercise him. Take him out for a long walk. Then, throw a tennis ball in the yard for a while. Try to tire him out as much as you can before you begin trimming his nails.

- **Location:** Some people prefer to trim their dog's nails on the sofa, because they feel the dog is more relaxed there. Others trim their dog's nails in the same area where they do the rest of their grooming. This is an individual choice.

- **Equipment:** There are a few pieces of equipment that you will need for trimming your dog's nails. You will need a nail clipper

Taking care of your Aussie's nails on a weekly basis is important.

of medium weight, styptic powder, cotton swabs, and treats.

- There are two types of nail clippers. The guillotine-style is named for its design. With this type of clipper, a metal edge comes out from one side and then cuts across the nail. The other kind of nail clipper is a scissors-style clipper, where both sides of the blade move toward the center. Many people prefer the scissors clipper because they contend that it distributes the pressure more evenly and results in a more even cut. You may wish to talk to your veterinarian about which type of nail clippers to use.

- **Inspect:** Before you actually begin trimming your dog's nails, you'll want to inspect them. Make sure that your dog has not broken any of his nails. Also look at the nail bed (the area at the base of the nail where it grows out of the skin), which should have hair. If you see red skin or puffiness, this could indicate a nail bed infection, which should be treated by your veterinarian. Also, note if the nails are wearing down evenly. If one nail is much longer than the adjacent nails, this could mean that your dog has a problem with how he is moving (which you should also discuss with your veterinarian). The nails are generally white, black, or both. Trimming white nails is easier because you can see where you are cutting.

- **Where to Cut:** The object is to trim some of the length off the end of the dog's nail, which is similar to trimming your own fingernails. The nail of a dog has a dead outer layer—this is the part that you cut. The middle of the nail has a blood vessel known as the quick that you do not want to cut, as it will cause pain and bleeding. You can usually see this in white nails but not in black ones. This is the reason you

cut slowly and make successive small cuts, ending before you get to the quick.

- **Take Your Time:** Eventually, it will take you less than five minutes to trim all your dog's nails. Initially, however, it will take much longer. Just take your time about the whole process until your dog becomes comfortable with it.

- **Be Confident:** It is important that your overall demeanor is one of confidence. If you act apprehensive or unsure, your dog will become nervous. You must act like trimming nails is a matter-of-fact part of life.

- **Make One Small Clip:** Gently but firmly pick up one foot in your left hand. Hold back the hair as much as possible around the first nail you want to trim. Using your right hand, make a very small clip off the end of the nail.

Scissors-style nail clippers are one option for trimming your Aussie's nails.

- **Make Several More Small Clips:** You can then make a few more very small clips on this same nail. The idea is to remove the part of the nail that starts to curve.
- **Treat:** After you do this first nail, let your dog know he is a good dog by praising him and giving him a treat.
- **Repeat with the Rest of the Nails on the Same Foot:** You have now trimmed one nail on one foot of your dog. Repeat these steps to complete the rest of the nails on the same foot.
- **Continue with the Rest of the Dog's Feet:** At this point, you have clipped all the nails on one foot. Repeat these steps for the rest of the nails on your dog's remaining feet.
- **Take a Break:** If your dog becomes apprehensive, you may want to take a break. Finish that particular nail, and then let your dog relax for a bit. However, it is important not to take a break until you actually finish that particular nail. You need to decide when to take a break, not your dog.
- **Avoid Cutting the Quick:** As you progress, you will start to see a white dot in the center of the nail. This white dot is the quick. You do not want to cut the quick, because it will hurt your dog. The time to stop trimming is when you see the quick.
- **If You Accidentally Cut the Quick:** At some time or another, many people accidentally cut the quick. If you do, the nail will begin to bleed. While it seems as if there is a lot of blood, in reality there are probably only a few drops. The most important thing to remember if you cut the quick is to remain calm. If you panic, the chances are that your dog will panic along with you. Put some styptic powder on a cotton swab. Then gently put the cotton swab around the nail and hold it firmly. You should also give your dog a treat so he's not afraid of nail trimming in the future.

FEET TRIMMING

An Australian Shepherd's feet also need weekly trimming. Hair grows out from the footpads, and left untrimmed, some dogs may slip on it.

How to Trim Your Dog's Feet

- **Location:** You will find it easiest to trim your dog's feet in the same place that you cut his nails. Cut his nails first and then trim his feet.
- **Equipment:** You will need 7-inch (18-cm) scissors and some treats.
- **Inspect:** Inspect your Aussie's feet. You want to make sure that his pads are in good shape without cuts.
- **Scissor the Hair:** Hold a foot in your left hand. Pick up the scissors in your right hand. In one continuous stroke, cut the excess hair growing out from each toe. Then cut any extra hair growing out from the pads. The overall look should be neat and tidy.
- **Repeat with Each Foot:** Trim each foot individually. After you finish the first foot, repeat these steps with the other three feet.

Want to Know More?

For advice on how to groom a senior Aussie, see Chapter 13: Care of Your Australian Shepherd Senior.

- **Treat:** After each foot is finished, tell your Aussie he is good and give him a treat.

DENTAL CARE

Dental care is important for your dog's overall health. Teeth problems can lead to much bigger health issues, including (in extreme cases) heart trouble. One of the best things you can do for your dog is to brush his teeth at least once a week, or even twice a week as some owners prefer.

How to Care for Your Dog's Teeth

- **Location:** You may want to brush your dog's teeth in your same general grooming area, though some people prefer to brush their dog's teeth in the kitchen. Keeping the tooth care equipment in plain view in the kitchen may help to remind you to brush his teeth.
- **Equipment:** Veterinary offices and most pet stores carry several types of toothpaste specially formulated for dogs. You cannot use human toothpaste, because it is not good for your dog and will, at a minimum, be an unpleasant experience for both of you. You can also buy toothbrushes made for dogs. Alternatively, you can use large gauze squares wrapped around your index finger. Also have some treats handy.
- **Inspect:** The first thing to do is visually inspect your dog's teeth. Make sure that they are white—not black, which indicates a dead tooth—and that none are missing or broken. Your dog's gums should be a healthy rose color, and he should not have any bumps in his mouth. Smell your dog's breath. If you smell a distinctly foul odor, your dog could have an infection in his mouth and should see a veterinarian.
- **Apply the Dog Toothpaste:** Apply the recommended amount of dog toothpaste to the toothbrush. If you are using gauze,

make a "toothbrush" by wrapping the gauze around the index finger you are most comfortable using, and apply the toothpaste to that. Again, it is important to use dog toothpaste, because human toothpaste is not good for dogs.

- **Lift Your Dog's Lip:** Move your dog's lip out of the way with your opposite hand.
- **Brush or Wipe Your Dog's Teeth:** Gently rub the toothbrush or your gauze-covered finger across your dog's teeth. Remember to do the outside and the inside of both the upper and lower rows of teeth.
- **Treat:** When you finish brushing your dog's teeth, tell him he is a good dog and then reward him with a treat.

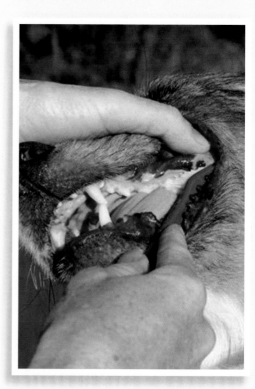

You should brush your Aussie's teeth at least once a week.

HOW TO FIND A PROFESSIONAL GROOMER

If you have never groomed an Australian Shepherd before, you may want to visit a professional groomer first. Ask the groomer if you can watch her groom your dog. That way, you will see exactly how you should groom your Aussie.

To find a professional groomer, rely on references or word of mouth. Start by asking your breeder (if your breeder is local) for a recommendation. You can also ask your veterinarian. Many modern veterinarians have grooming facilities associated with their practice. Your neighbors may also use professional groomers and can give you some suggestions.

The main thing about selecting a groomer is that you really want her to be a professional. If you find a potential groomer, visit the shop. Make sure that the facility is adequate and clean. Observe the groomer while she is actually grooming to see if she is gentle. Look at several dogs after they have been groomed to make sure that they look nice. Ask the groomer about her fees, what shampoos and conditioners she uses, and any other questions you may have. Since you will visit your groomer often, it is easier to choose one who is close to where you live.

BEYOND BASIC GROOMING SKILLS

You may discover that you truly love grooming your Australian Shepherd. Some people find grooming to be extremely relaxing and highly enjoyable. If you are one of these people, you may want to learn more-advanced grooming skills. Also, if you want to show your Australian Shepherd, you may want to learn how to groom him sufficiently to present him in the breed ring.

If so, several options are available to you. The best option is for you to ask your breeder if you could visit her and watch her groom. Most breeders would be happy to teach owners of dogs that they bred how to groom their dogs. If you get a grooming lesson from your breeder, it is considerate to bring her a small thank-you gift for her time.

Another option is to go to a local dog show. Your breeder can help you find one. If you arrive about two hours ahead of the time that Australian Shepherds will be showing, you can observe many handlers grooming their show dogs. Some of them may be willing to give you a quick lesson at that time. Others may be willing to help you after they have finished showing for the day.

Still another option would be to attend a grooming seminar. Most local breed clubs, which your breeder can tell you about, offer educational seminars. A common seminar is one for advanced grooming, especially for the show ring.

CHAPTER 7

AUSTRALIAN SHEPHERD NUTRITIONAL NEEDS

As with any dogs, Australian Shepherds have certain nutritional needs that are different from those of people. Good nutrition is essential to maintain the health and well-being of your dog. A healthy dog is a happy dog.

To understand your dog's nutritional needs, you'll need to learn about the building blocks of basic nutrition, including carbohydrates, fats, proteins, minerals, vitamins, and water. You must also decide what type of food to give your Aussie. There are a variety of dog food choices available, including commercial foods, noncommercial foods, and special diets. Plus, every dog needs some treats and bones!

WHY IS GOOD NUTRITION SO ESSENTIAL?

Good nutrition is essential to maintaining your Australian Shepherd's overall health, thereby ensuring that he lives as long as possible. If your dog has a dense, shiny coat; clear, pink skin; and sparkling eyes, chances are that you are meeting his nutritional needs. If not, then you may want to reconsider what you are feeding him. Many people also examine their dog's feces to determine if he's getting the right nutrition. Firm feces are fine, but loose stools may indicate otherwise.

The nutritional requirements for a healthy dog include many of the same components as those for people. The difference, however, is largely in the amount of each component. The stomach of a dog is far smaller, relatively speaking, than the stomach of a person.

Further, as a double-coated breed, Australian Shepherds require a certain amount of fat intake to keep their coat healthy. The protein-to-fat ratio in food is a big concern to many owners, but Aussies definitely need some fat in their diet to maintain their glorious coat. However, there is little agreement on just how much fat to feed your dog and also what the ratio of protein to fat should be.

The nutritional requirements of a dog vary over time. A growing puppy needs certain components, whereas an adult dog needs fewer of them. A senior dog may need even fewer than an adult.

The entire subject of good nutrition can get involved, and it's up to you to do your research. Most people have a thorough discussion with their veterinarian about good nutrition when they get their dog and indeed

A good diet provides your Aussie with the energy he needs for staying fit and healthy.

throughout the various stages of his life. Your breeder probably has definite thoughts on the subject too. You can also surf the Net for good articles about nutrition, from the basics to factors that are more advanced. Certain dog publications also provide annual listings of various dog foods, including their nutritional values; some even rank these dog foods.

THE BUILDING BLOCKS OF NUTRITION

Every dog needs certain nutritional building blocks, including carbohydrates, fats, proteins, minerals, vitamins, and water. All these building blocks must be in the proper balance to each other and must be given to your dog in the proper amounts. If you give too much or too little of any one, your dog may get very

sick. The overall balance is extremely delicate, and too much interference, even with the best of intentions, can prove ruinous for your dog's health.

The old saying "you are what you eat" is just as true for dogs; a dog also is what he eats. No matter what you eventually decide to feed your dog, you should consider whether or not that food includes a balanced amount of all these basic building blocks.

Carbohydrates

Carbohydrates are organic compounds that can occur in starch form, such as cereals or sugars. Their formulations can be either simple or complex. Simple carbohydrates include fruit and sugar; complex carbohydrates include whole grains. Carbohydrates are an important source of energy for all living creatures, including dogs. You can think of carbohydrates as helping to provide your dog with fuel. Carbohydrates are also necessary for tissue and cell formation. For dogs, sources of carbohydrates include grains such as corn, rice, wheat, and oats. Other sources of carbohydrates can be certain vegetables and even soybeans.

There is currently a controversy regarding whether or not dogs should be fed grains. Some people insist that no dogs should be fed any grain—that it is mere filler with minimal nutritional value, and that dogs should be fed an almost pure protein diet. Others argue that grains are necessary for dogs because wild dogs first rip open and eat the stomach of their prey, and the stomach contains mainly grains. As with any controversy regarding your dog's health, the matter of whether or not to feed your dog grains is something to discuss at length with your veterinarian.

Fats

Fats are another basic building block for good dog nutrition. Fats are also referred to as oils or lipids, depending on their state; oils are fats that are in liquid form. Fats can be found in chicken, meat (such as beef), and fish (such as salmon). They are also found in some plants (such as soybeans). Oils derived from canola, flaxseed, olives, trout, and salmon also contain fats.

Fats are important because they can help protect vital organs and also generally insulate and protect the dog's body. They are necessary for good skin and coat development and are also a source of energy. In reasonable quantities, fat also just makes food taste better. Indeed, fats are necessary for overall health. Dogs can produce some fats, but they need additional essential fatty acids from their food. These essential fatty acids include omega 3 and omega 6. Of course, too much fat in a dog's diet will result in obesity, which will be discussed at the end of this chapter.

Proteins

Proteins are organic compounds composed of long strings of amino acids in different sequences. Amino acids are considered to be the building blocks of life. As such, proteins are necessary for almost every bodily process and help convert food into energy. They also help

Fish is a good source of protein.

maintain a dog's overall immune system and the health of his basic tissues, bones, muscles, skin, teeth, and nails. Some proteins are known as enzymes, which start chemical reactions involved in basic metabolism.

Dogs need to obtain some of their protein from their diet; they cannot manufacture enough protein themselves. Accordingly, dogs get most of their protein by eating foods with protein, including beef, fish, eggs, chicken, turkey, duck, dairy, lamb, and bison. Dogs are better able to absorb protein derived from animal-based sources than those derived from plant-based sources, like soy.

Minerals

Minerals are substances with specific chemical compositions that are found naturally occurring in nature. Some are very complex, and others are very simple in structure. While dogs do not need large amounts, they do require minute amounts of certain minerals as part of a balanced diet, because they cannot manufacture these minerals themselves.

Minerals are necessary for your dog's overall health, including his immune system, bones, blood, muscles, and nervous system. Some minerals that dogs require include calcium, iron, potassium, magnesium, selenium, copper, phosphorus, and zinc. Most dog food labels contain a lengthy list of small quantities of minerals that have been added to the basic food.

Vitamins

Vitamins, like minerals, are organic chemical compounds necessary for a dog's balanced nutrition. Vitamins are necessary for a dog's nervous system, good bones, nice coat, and eyes. Dogs need vitamins A, B, D, E, and K.

Vitamins can be either water soluble or fat soluble. With water-soluble vitamins, such as

Training Tidbit

You can train your Aussie to sit before receiving his food. Teaching him to sit before you set down his food bowl will make him more polite and manageable during feeding times.

vitamin C, any excess amounts are passed in the urine. Fat-soluble vitamins, like vitamin E, are stored in fat, if there is any excess. It is dangerous to overdose a dog with fat-soluble vitamins.

Some vitamins are absorbed only up to certain quantities within a particular period of time. Because of this, some are available in time-release formulas, such as vitamin B. Other vitamins, notably vitamin C, may have buffering agents to protect the dog's stomach, as it tends to be acidic.

Water

Water is composed of two hydrogen molecules and one oxygen molecule. Water is necessary for all life. While a dog could do without food for a while, he would quickly die without water. Water is absolutely essential for every single process in your dog's body.

Accordingly, you should always provide your dog with adequate and clean water. You cannot change your dog's water bowl too often. Most people use tap water when home. However, when traveling, you may want to bring bottled water, since some locations may rely on well water or other sources. In any event, you should always bring a supply of fresh water when you take your dog out. If it is hot outside, you may need to offer your dog some water during your daily walks. You can purchase a portable water bottle for this purpose. You do not want your dog to drink from a stagnant pond that may contain contaminants.

If your dog suddenly stops drinking water, he may be seriously ill. Similarly, if your dog begins to drink copious amounts of water, he may also be very ill. Either way, you should consult your veterinarian.

WHAT TO FEED YOUR AUSTRALIAN SHEPHERD

Deciding what to feed your Australian Shepherd is an important and difficult decision. There are many options available. Currently, as with the issue of vaccinations, what to feed your dog is controversial—in part because of the abundance of options. The most common options include commercial foods, noncommercial foods, and special diets. Commercial foods include dry food (kibble), semi-moist food, and canned food. Noncommercial foods include home-cooked diets and raw diets. Special diets include both prescription diets and various supplements. All these options will be discussed below.

The Current Dog Food Controversy

Not too long ago, selecting food for your dog was a relatively simple matter. You just went to the local grocery store and selected from a few different brands of kibble and maybe chose a can or two. Dog food was essentially mass-produced in commercial qualities. Lately, however, there has been a revolution in the types of food available for dogs.

Today, a wide group of dog owners believe that dogs should be feed only holistic food. The problem is that there is not a universally accepted—or regulated—definition of what "holistic," "natural," or "organic" food means for people or dogs. At the very least, food purporting to be holistic should be made from ingredients fit for human consumption; it should not have pet-grade ingredients. Further, holistic food should be free from any antibiotics, meaning that the protein source (chicken, lamb, buffalo, salmon, etc.) wasn't exposed to any antibiotics during its lifetime. Last, holistic food should be hormone-free, meaning that these same protein sources were not given any hormones.

Many dog owners who use holistic food also firmly believe that the ingredients should come from suppliers within the United States, as our regulations are stricter than those of most other countries. In addition, owners demand that the holistic food be manufactured in this country as well. Many also want the manufactures of a particular brand of food to have their own specific manufacturing plant. Should you choose the holistic route, it is well worth researching whether or not a particular holistic brand is made in the same manufacturing plant as pet-grade brands.

Supplements are also a controversial subject. Some owners firmly believe that a quality food does not require additional supplements or vitamins. There are also those who strongly feel that all foods benefit from additional supplements or vitamins.

You should definitely schedule time with your veterinarian to help you decide what to feed your Aussie.

Want to Know More?

To find out what to feed your puppy, see Chapter 3: Care of Your Australian Shepherd Puppy. To find out what to feed your senior, see Chapter 13: Care of Your Australian Shepherd Senior.

Commercial dog foods are easy to find and use.

Whatever you decide, buy the best-quality dog food that you can afford.

Commercial Dog Food

The main advantage of commercial dog food is that it is easy to find and easy to use—all you have to do is buy it. There are many places where you can buy commercial dog food, including grocery stores, pet stores, veterinarians, groomers, boarding kennels, and the Internet.

Commercial dog foods are available in three different forms: dry food, semi-moist food, and canned food.

Dry Food

Dry dog food comes in a bag and is often referred to as kibble. It is the most economical and the easiest way to feed your dog. Plus, chewing on the hard kibble is good for cleaning a dog's teeth. The companies that manufacture dog food conduct research and decide what constitutes a balanced diet and prepare it in a dry form.

Dry dog food is easily stored in a bin, but you should keep it covered and out of the reach of your dog. If not, chances are that your Australian Shepherd will find it and eat all the food, which could contribute to a life-threatening condition known as bloat.

Dry dog food has its detractors—people who believe that it is not healthy for dogs. However, there are a plethora of companies that offer kibble made from hormone-free and antibiotic-free protein sources. Many companies use only range-free meat sources as well. Often the protein sources are uncommon, like duck, buffalo, or salmon. These types of unusual proteins can be good for dogs with allergies. The general theory is that a dog may be allergic to a more common protein source but may tolerate a more exotic one. Some people feel that baked kibble preserves more of the nutrition and is more easily digested. In any event, a holistic kibble should not have any chemical preservatives; it should be naturally preserved. Holistic kibble should not contain any artificial colors or flavors. Many holistic kibbles do not contain wheat or rice gluten or any other inexpensive by-products or cheap fillers.

Semi-Moist Food

Semi-moist foods come in pouches and are available wherever dry dog foods are found. By definition, they have higher water content than dry food. They also have more preservatives in order to remain edible. Most people do not use semi-moist foods as the mainstay of their dog's diet; however, semi-moist foods are useful as training tools when portioned out appropriately, as dogs tend to love the taste. They are also useful if your dog is slightly off his food and needs to be tempted to eat.

Canned Food

Canned food is food that comes in a can. Like semi-moist food, it has higher water content and more preservatives than dry food does but less than semi-moist food. A spoonful of canned food may be a good source of additional fat for your dog or may tempt a finicky eater. However, most people do not feed their dogs a steady diet of canned food. You can find holistic canned food available as well.

Reading the Label

Take time to study the label of any commercially available food, whether or not it's called "holistic." The label will tell you what is in the food. The ingredients are listed by highest percentage of quantity in the product in descending order. However, similar ingredients may be split in order to make them look like a lower percentage of the whole, making the food labels difficult to read. For example, different forms of corn, such as ground corn and corn gluten, may be listed separately to lower the individual percentage of each, thereby making them appear lower on the ingredient list. If they were combined, then they may have outweighed the protein and would then have appeared as the first ingredient, making the food look less nutritious. Any preservatives or food coloring used in the product will also be indicated on the label.

A spoonful of canned food may be a good source of additional fat for your dog or may tempt a finicky eater.

Most manufacturers of commercial dog foods maintain websites where they carefully describe their food. They list and discuss all the ingredients and often provide a customer service number for you to call if you have any questions.

Changing It Up

Because of the wide range of choices in dog foods today, some people think that a dog's food should be changed every six months to a year. Others believe that if a particular commercial brand offers different protein sources, then the protein source should be changed every six months to a year. For example, if Brand X offers a chicken variety and a salmon variety, they would feed the chicken variety for six months and then switch to the salmon variety for the next six months.

If you decide to change your Aussie's food, do it slowly.

If you decide to change the type of food or brand of food, do it slowly. Mix the two foods together over the course of one week. At first, just use the original food. Then slowly increase the amount of the new food while decreasing the amount of the original food. By the end of one week, you will be feeding your Aussie only the new food. This method applies to any change in type or brand of food, for both young and adult dogs. If you switch too quickly to a new brand or type of food, your dog will more than likely get diarrhea.

Noncommercial Dog Food

With the advent of so many noncommercial dog diets, many people are opting to feed them to their dogs. This is especially true given the recent dog food recalls across just about the full spectrum of commercial dog foods. Types of noncommercial dog diets include home-cooked and raw diets. While many people believe in the health benefits of these diets, feeding noncommercial dog foods requires a lot of preparation and is much more expensive than relying on a commercial dog food.

Home-Cooked Diet

Those who favor the use of holistic food often prefer to home-cook for their dog. In its purest form, with a home-cooked diet, you cook your dog's food in your own home. If you decide to go this route, be especially mindful of a dog's nutritional requirements and that they change as the dog matures. You should consult a veterinarian on this point.

The advantage of home cooking is that you know exactly what ingredients are in the food and where they come from. You can buy all the ingredients for your dog's food in a local holistic grocery store. However, a disadvantage is that home cooking can be time-consuming. You would be preparing

The advantage to a raw food diet is that you know exactly what you are feeding your dog.

batches of food on almost a daily basis. Another disadvantage can be the cost. Also, it makes traveling with your dog much more difficult.

There are several commercially available home-cooked diets. With these, you purchase a bag of freeze-dried, home-cooked food and then add a meat source in the proper amount as indicated on the bag. It is a simple matter to cook the meat source, add water, and then mix in the freeze-dried food.

Raw Diet

Many dog owners feel that a good alternative to the home-cooked diet is the raw food diet. Followers of this school believe that this diet is best because wild dogs ate only raw food. Therefore, our dogs today should be fed only raw food because that is their "natural" diet. The diet consists of several types of raw meat and bones together with certain supplements.

The advantage to a raw food diet is that you know exactly what you are feeding your dog.

The disadvantage is that people often buy the raw meat and bones in bulk to cut down on the cost and therefore need a dedicated freezer. In addition, traveling with your dog can be hard if he's on this diet.

Some companies now offer a type of raw food diet on a commercial basis. The food is already prepared for you. Some companies offer raw diets in frozen logs, which you slice off to accommodate your Aussie's needs. Other companies offer raw diets in freeze-dried form, which, although more expensive, makes traveling a lot easier. Commercially prepared raw food diets are more expensive than a raw food diet prepared by you, because they save you time. However, for many, the cost can be almost prohibitive—especially if you have multiple dogs. There are also those who fear that a raw diet may expose the dog to illness; specifically, certain raw foods may contain bacteria such as E. coli or salmonella.

Special Diets

Certain companies make special diets in dry and canned forms available from veterinarians and only by prescription. A veterinarian may prescribe a special diet if a dog has a certain health condition indicative of the need for a special diet. These health conditions can include kidney disease, allergies, and obesity. Your veterinarian will let you know if your dog needs to be on a prescription diet. If so, it may be that your dog needs to eat the prescription diet only until his condition resolves. For example, if you properly diet your dog down to a healthy weight, then he may not need to continue to be on a prescription diet for obesity.

Supplements

There are two types of supplements. The first type is commercially available and may

Multi-Dog Tip

Bones can be a special treat but can also be overly exciting to dogs. If you have multiple dogs, you can prevent any arguments between them by offering each of them a bone in their crate.

also be holistic in nature. In effect, these are additional vitamins and minerals for your dog. They can be in the form of an overall supplement consisting of a variety of additional vitamins and minerals. Many of these are extremely palatable to dogs, who simply eat them with their food. Alternatively, some of these supplements are available in a pure form consisting of only that particular supplement. For example, some people feed a little additional salmon oil for the extra omega 3 and omega 6 fatty acids. These supplements can be especially useful after your Aussie sheds to help his skin retain its normal moisture.

The other type of supplementation consists of particular foods that you may choose to add to your dog's diet, especially if you are feeding your dog a commercial diet. For example, on occasion, some people add a hard-cooked egg, yogurt, or cottage cheese to their dog's kibble.

Other people add a few blueberries or even some oatmeal from time to time.

If you decide to supplement your dog's food, be sure to ask your vet first to ensure that you are maintaining a balanced diet overall for your dog. She will advise you about what to give, how much, and how often.

Treats and Bones

Every dog deserves to have treats and bones. Australian Shepherds are very food motivated, so treats are invaluable training tools. Treats are especially important when first training an exercise, but treats are always helpful even for training experienced dogs.

Treats are available in all forms. Any grocery store or pet store has many commercially available treats. Some are dry, some are semi-moist, and others are very moist. Many of these are also holistic in nature. If you use holistic dry food, the manufacturer of that food probably also offers associated treats.

In addition, you can use some types of human food that are safe to feed your dog. Many people like to use beef jerky, small pieces of hot dogs, and even cheese for treats. Some dogs even think that uncooked macaroni is a wonderful treat. Most dogs, as with most people, prefer a variety of treats rather than the same one all the time.

If you decide to give your dog a bone as a

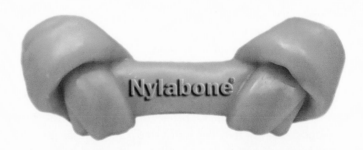

Nylabone makes chews that are safe for strong chewers.

treat, it is safer to offer him either a raw bone, such as a knuckle bone, or a smoked bone. Many veterinarians advise that you not give your dog a cooked bone, as they are more likely to splinter. Also, many vets prefer that you give your dog only large bones, such as knuckle bones, since smaller bones (like chicken bones) can splinter—even if they are raw. Australian Shepherds are serious chewers, especially when they are young and teething. Some commercially available chews, like the ones Nylabone makes, are safe for these big-time chewers.

WHEN TO FEED AN ADULT DOG

You have now made the difficult and complicated decision of *what* to feed your dog. Now you have to decide *when* to feed your adult dog, and how many times a day you will feed him.

How Many Times a Day

It is possible to feed your adult Australian Shepherd only once a day. However, most people feed their adult dog twice a day. Australian Shepherds, for the most part, truly love their food. It makes them happier when you split their meals in half and feed them twice a day

What Times of Day

As with puppies, your adult Australian Shepherd should be fed at approximately the same time(s) every day. It is easiest to feed your dog his breakfast when you eat your breakfast and his dinner when you eat your dinner.

OBESITY

As mentioned earlier, Australian Shepherds are very fond of food. Some of them are so fond of food that they become obese. Obesity in dogs must be controlled by the owner—it is your responsibility. If your dog becomes obese, it's your fault.

Obesity decreases the lifespan of your dog. It will also seriously and negatively impact the quality of his life. Obesity puts additional and unnecessary pressure on joints, thereby increasing the likelihood and severity of arthritis.

How can you tell if your Aussie is at the proper weight? First, you can tell by looking at him. The front of your dog should be approximately as wide as his rear, with no bulging stomach in between. Also, perhaps the best test of proper weight is that you should be able to feel your dog's ribs if you lightly touch his ribcage.

If you suspect that your dog is obese, you will need to reduce his food slowly over time. Some people add cooked green beans to supplement the smaller portions. In any event, your veterinarian will help you develop an appropriate diet plan.

By the Numbers

Always let your adult dog outside after you have fed him. Adult dogs need schedules too. This way, he will learn to eliminate after being fed.

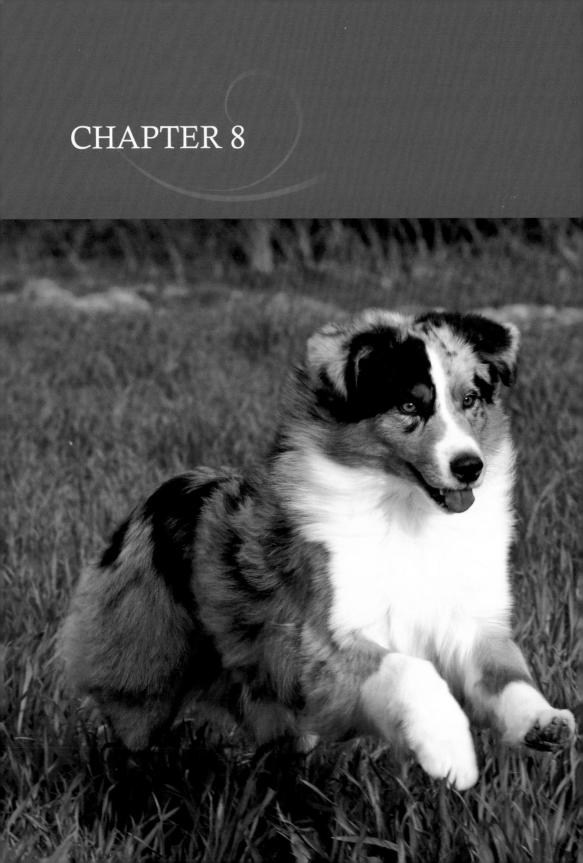

CHAPTER 8

AUSTRALIAN SHEPHERD HEALTH AND WELLNESS

Overall, Australian Shepherds are a healthy breed. However, there are certain things you can do to help keep your dog healthy, such as an annual veterinarian examination and preventing internal and external parasites. In addition, you should be aware of certain breed-specific illnesses, such as juvenile cataracts, hip dysplasia, hypothyroidism, epilepsy, hemangiosarcoma, and lymphosarcoma, and certain generic health issues, including allergies, ear infections, and eye infections.

ANNUAL VETERINARIAN EXAM

To make sure that your Australian Shepherd remains fit and healthy, you should take him for an annual veterinarian exam. After age eight, you should take him twice a year. As with people, if problems are caught and treated early enough, many do not become serious.

At the annual exam, your veterinarian will first weigh your dog and then check the records to see if he has gained or lost weight. Any significant loss in weight could be a sign of poor health or even a disease such as cancer. By the same token, a large increase in weight may show that your dog has become obese.

Your veterinarian will then examine your dog. She will take your dog's temperature, look into his eyes and ears, and feel his body. She will listen to your dog's heartbeat and check the color of his skin. She will also check your dog's teeth and let you know if they need to be cleaned professionally or if any teeth require extraction.

Most vets will then ask if you have noticed any changes in your dog's overall behavior. She will ask if your dog is eating as well as ever and if your dog is drinking a lot more or a lot less water. She will also ask if you have seen any increase or decrease in elimination or any associated changes with elimination habits. She will ask if you have noticed any problem behaviors such as excessive barking, chewing, digging, or aggression.

Your veterinarian will also ask if you have

Want to Know More?

Problem behaviors will be addressed in Chapter 10: Australian Shepherd Problem Behaviors.

To make sure that your Australian Shepherd remains fit and healthy, you should take him for an annual veterinarian exam.

the first signs of impending health problems. In addition, you should also bring in a fecal sample to allow the vet to check for internal parasites.

At the conclusion of your dog's annual examination, your veterinarian will probably ask you if you have any concerns or questions. If she does not ask, then speak up and ask her about anything concerning your dog's health during this visit. This is your time with your veterinarian to address any issues you may have about your dog and how best to keep him healthy and happy.

Office Etiquette

There is a certain etiquette you should follow when at your veterinarian's office. First, your dog should always be on a leash. And you should always have the leash very short so that your dog cannot inadvertently jump onto a person or another dog. Ideally, your dog should be kept on leash right by your side while in the waiting room. Although your dog is most likely healthy, many other dogs in the veterinarian's waiting room are there because they are sick. Keep a safe distance from other dogs and cats—for their sakes and for your dog's sake. Of course, if your dog eliminates on his way into or out of the veterinarian's office, be sure to properly clean up after him.

PARASITES

All parasites feed off of their host, and if your dog is the host, it can weaken him. If left unchecked, they can make your dog extremely ill. Parasites can be both internal and external.

Internal Parasites

Internal parasites exist inside a host's body. Heartworms live inside a dog's heart; hookworms, roundworms, tapeworms, and whipworms live inside a dog's intestinal tract.

maintained appropriate parasite prevention, which will be discussed later in this chapter, and she may ask if you require more parasite prevention medication. If your dog is currently on any other medication, she will ask if you need refills. If this is your dog's first annual examination after receiving all the puppy vaccinations, and if your dog has not yet been spayed or neutered, your veterinarian will probably discuss spaying or neutering your dog.

Once a year, it is a good idea for the veterinarian to draw both blood and urine. Full blood panels and urine analyses are often

These latter types of worms produce eggs that are passed through the dog's feces—other dogs may become infected if the feces are not picked up. A dog may become infected with any or all of these internal parasites on a recurring basis. Since most of the heartworm preventatives also prevent common intestinal worm infestations, giving your dog monthly heartworm preventative goes a long way toward eliminating most of these internal parasites. Additionally, keeping your yard clean of feces also helps to prevent infections.

Heartworms

Mosquitoes are carriers of heartworm disease. If you live in an area prone to mosquitoes, then you especially need to give your dog heartworm preventative. When a mosquito bites an infected dog and then bites a second dog, the mosquito transmits the heartworm larvae from the infected dog to the second dog. As the name implies, heartworms attack a dog's heart and also his lungs. They can block a dog's arteries as well. Eventually, the blood vessel and heart blockages lead to heart failure.

Signs of heartworms include a general failure to thrive. Infected dogs are listless, have trouble breathing, lose weight, cough, and are generally tired. They can develop fluid around their heart, and their lungs and heart will not sound normal when listened to by a veterinarian.

Treatment of severe heartworm infestation can be as severe as the resulting disease—some dogs simply do not survive it. The treatment kills both the larvae and the adult heartworms, and the typical treatment medications used are macrocyclic lactone drugs and melarsomine, which are usually administered while the dog is hospitalized. As the heartworms die, they may further clog the heart. A dog undergoing heartworm treatment may even cough up blood. He must be watched very carefully and cannot be allowed to exercise. Any exercise will increase his blood circulation and thereby increase a possible blockage of arteries due to dead worms. Following release from the hospital, the dog must be closely monitored. After 30 days, he needs to be rechecked due to the high likelihood that larvae are still present. This check generally requires another hospitalization. There will be follow-up appointments on a regular basis to ensure that no larvae have returned. Retreatment may be required. Even if a dog survives heartworm treatment, his heart may be permanently weakened, and he may be more prone to congestive heart failure as a senior.

There is a fast blood test your veterinarian can perform that will indicate whether or not your dog has heartworm. This test should be performed on any adult dog you take into your home. It is not necessary for eight-week-old puppies.

By the Numbers

Once your dog reaches the age of one year, it is advisable to take him to the veterinarian for an annual wellness examination. This exam should also include a fecal analysis, full blood panel, and urinalysis. These tests will help you maintain your dog's overall good health. By the time your dog is an adult, you should be familiar with his general habits. If you notice any changes, take him to the veterinarian.

If you live in an area prone to mosquitoes, then you especially need to give your dog heartworm preventative.

Thankfully, it is easy to prevent heartworm, although infected dogs cannot be given any preventative until they are cured. The simple way to prevent heartworm is to give your Aussie a heartworm preventative, which comes as a pill that is dosed according to your dog's weight. Heartworm preventative should never be split among dogs—each dog should get his correct dosage of the correctly sized pill. Most heartworm preventatives are given once a month, and it is imperative that you not miss administering any single dosage.

There are several manufacturers of heartworm preventative, one of which uses ivermectin. Some individuals within certain breeds—including Australian Shepherds—may have a genetic mutation that makes then overly sensitive to some drugs, including ivermectin. You can purchase a brand of heartworm preventative that does not contain ivermectin. Alternatively, you can have your Australian Shepherd tested for this genetic mutation, which is called MDR1. The benefit of testing for the MDR1 mutation is that you will then know if your dog is sensitive to other drugs as well and can so inform your veterinarian. The test results will indicate if your dog has no copies, one copy, or two copies of this mutation. His sensitivity level increases with the number of copies of the mutation. If you decide to test your dog for the MDR1 mutation, contact Washington State University (www.vetmed. wsu.edu/depts-vcpl/).

Hookworms

Hookworms are one of the most common internal parasites in dogs, especially puppies, although older dogs may develop hookworm as well. There are different species of hookworms, including *Ancylostoma braziliense*, *Ancylostoma caninum*, *Ancylostoma tubaeforme*, and *Uncinaria stencephala*. The most common type found in dogs is *Ancylostoma caninum*, which also happens to be the most dangerous to dogs. Some of these species prefer colder climates while other types prefer warmer climates, but hookworms can be found just about anywhere in the country. They live in a dog's small intestine, where they feed on the dog's blood.

Hookworm larvae can pass through a mother's milk to her puppies. Dogs can also be infected through feces. Either way, an infected dog can pass millions of eggs, which stay alive for several months.

A dog with hookworms may have blood in his stool, bloody diarrhea, or pale gums. He may also lose weight, pass blackish or tar-like feces, and be generally lethargic. Because

Heartworm Preventative

Heartworm can be a deadly, expensive disease. The good news is that heartworm is easily prevented by giving your Aussie a monthly heartworm pill available from your veterinarian. This preventative helps protect against certain other types of worms as well.

hookworms feed on the dog's blood, a dog infested with hookworms can become anemic. A veterinarian can test a dog's stool sample for the presence of hookworms.

If your Aussie has hookworm infection, he can be treated with one of several deworming products available from your veterinarian. The treatment is given in two doses a few weeks apart. The medication kills only the adult worms, not the larvae or eggs, so the second treatment is used to kill the larvae that matured into adults since the initial dose. In severe cases, a dog may need a blood transfusion.

The good news is that the monthly

A monthly heartworm preventative will also largely protect against roundworms.

heartworm preventative generally also protects against hookworms. However, it is possible for a dog to get hookworms even if he is on heartworm preventative. For that reason, testing the dog's stool at least once or even twice a year is a good idea.

Roundworms

There are a vast number of different species of roundworms that infect dogs, but the two most common types are *Toxocara canis* and *Toxascaris leonina*, both of which can be transmitted to people. An infected mother dog can give her unborn puppies roundworms, and they can be passed through a dog's feces, too.

Dogs with roundworms may have a pot-bellied appearance and also cough, vomit, and have diarrhea. Veterinarians can diagnosis the presence of roundworms through a fecal examination.

The treatment is a medication given three days in a row; then the course of treatment is repeated about a month later. A monthly heartworm preventative will also largely protect against roundworms. As with other parasites, it is wise to keep your yard clean to avoid environmental contamination through feces.

Tapeworms

As their name implies, tapeworms are long, rather flat worms that grow up to 2 feet (61 cm) in length. A tapeworm consists of a head followed by many segments, each of which has egg sacs full of a tremendous amount of

Keeping your dog and your house clean are important measures for preventing external parasites.

eggs. Tapeworms attach themselves to a dog's intestines. A dog can get tapeworms by eating infected fleas, rabbits, or rodents. Any worm, including a tapeworm, deprives a dog of some nutrition.

Sometimes, you can tell if your dog has tapeworms because you will see small, rice-like objects in his feces or even stuck in the hair around his anus. These objects are segments of the tapeworm, which are actually egg sacs. If these segments are especially long, your dog may scoot his bottom along the ground after elimination.

A veterinarian can confirm the presence of tapeworms through a fecal analysis, but tapeworms don't always show up in fecal screening tests, so it is important to occasionally examine your dog's stools for evidence. If your dog has tapeworms, your veterinarian will prescribe an appropriate deworming medication. You may need to administer this medication at least twice to ensure that all worms have been eliminated.

A few heartworm preventatives protect against tapeworms. Further, it is important not to have fleas either on your dog or in your house. We will discuss flea control later in this chapter.

Whipworms

Whipworms are another type of worm that attaches itself to a dog's intestines. But unlike tapeworms, whipworms are very small. They live by ingesting their host's blood. A dog acquires whipworms by eating contaminated feces or by drinking contaminated water.

Signs of whipworm infestation include a general lethargy, anemia, a decrease in weight, passing gas, and bloody diarrhea. In excessive quantities, whipworms can cause internal bleeding.

A veterinarian can determine if a dog has whipworms through a fecal examination. However, it can be difficult to confirm their presence, because the veterinarian must actually find whipworm eggs in the feces. These eggs can be extremely small, shed intermittently in very small numbers, and may not be present in a particular fecal sample. When found, the veterinarian will prescribe a dewormer which, as with other dewormers, will likely have to be given several times. Some monthly heartworm preventatives protect against whipworms. However, as with other worms, keeping your yard clean of feces goes a long way toward preventing any infestation.

External Parasites

External parasites exist on the dog's body and even in your house. Keeping your dog and your house clean are important measures for preventing these parasites. The three most common types of external parasites are fleas, mites, and ticks.

Fleas

The type of flea most common in the United States is *Ctenocephalides felis*, or the domestic cat flea. They appear as dark brown to black specks. Although fleas cannot fly, they can jump almost 200 times the length of their body.

Fleas survive by biting a host, such as a dog, and then sucking the blood. Humans and cats can be bitten by fleas as well. In addition to itching tremendously, a flea bite can cause skin irritations. Some dogs (and even people) are allergic to a flea's saliva and may scratch themselves bloody. Dogs may lick off a spot of hair surrounding the bite. The skin can turn red and ooze, in which case it becomes what is known as a hot spot. In severe cases, a flea-infested dog can develop anemia.

Fleas can be largely prevented through the use of a topical preventative that contains insecticide that kills both the fleas and their larvae.

If your dog has fleas, you will have to conduct an all-out assault to eliminate them. You should first bathe your dog, preferably in a shampoo specially formulated to soothe skin, such as an oatmeal-based shampoo. After drying your dog, comb him out. Then use a flea comb, which is an even smaller comb with very short, close prongs that can catch the fleas. Once you comb out a flea, immediately drown it in a glass of soapy water or alcohol. You will also have to thoroughly wash all the bedding in the house—yours and the dog's—in hot water. Be sure to include any throws placed over furniture or beds as well. Last, you must vacuum your entire house very thoroughly. With severe infestations, you may need to vacuum your house on a daily basis until the fleas are eliminated. Some people apply borax

overnight to their rugs and then vacuum. If you use this method, do not allow your dog to walk on the rugs until the borax has been removed.

Consult with your veterinarian about products that will both kill and prevent fleas. Certain products kill adult fleas; others, called insect growth regulators, or IGRs, stop immature fleas from developing into adults, which prevents them from reproducing. These products are available in several forms, including dips, shampoos, topical sprays, and powders. Some of these products contain insecticide, while others are based on pyrethrins, derived from chrysanthemums.

Fleas can be largely prevented through the use of a topical preventative that contains insecticide that kills both the fleas and their larvae. This topical is liquid and is applied to a dog's back between his shoulder blades. Usually, the medication is used once every one to three months. There are some owners who prefer less harsh measures, such as brewer's yeast, garlic, or apple cider vinegar. Some people claim success using natural oils derived from pennyroyal, lavender, eucalyptus, or citronella. However, these more natural preventatives may not be as effective, especially against more severe flea infestations. Flea collars are not recommended, as many dogs are allergic or at least sensitive to them. Also, an Australian Shepherd could get his flea collar stuck onto something and choke.

Mites

Certain microscopic parasitic mites can cause mange. There are two types of mange: The first is sarcoptic mange (or canine scabies) and is caused by the *Sarcoptes scabei* mite; the second type is demodectic mange and is caused by

Aussies are considered to be a generally healthy breed.

the *Demodex canis* mite. Each type of mange is treated differently.

Sarcoptic mange is highly contagious between dogs. Signs of sarcoptic mange include pronounced scratching, which often leads to scabs, sores, and hair loss. Usually, you will see signs of sarcoptic mange around a dog's face—especially his ears—and also on his abdomen, legs, and elbows. If untreated, this type of mange will spread over the dog's body.

Demodectic mange is caused by mites that are already present on your dog's skin. For most dogs, these demodectic mange mites do not cause any problem. However, in the case of an already compromised immune system, demodectic mange can become more difficult to cure. A mother can pass these mites to her puppies. The sign of demodectic mange is small hair loss, usually around the paws. The area can be red or dotted with red spots and is usually scaly. In most cases, demodectic mange will resolve itself over time. If not, your dog should be examined for immune deficiencies as well as for hypothyroidism, or low thyroid. Some dogs develop secondary bacterial infections at the infection site. Demodectic mange is generally found in young dogs and puppies. Consequently, adult dogs who develop demodectic mange should be checked for immune deficiencies or other underlying medical problems.

If you see signs of either type of mange, take your dog to his veterinarian for a skin scraping. This will determine if your dog has mange and, if so, which type of mange is present. Dogs with sarcoptic mange must be kept apart from other dogs. All dogs in your household should also be treated. Treatment for both types of mange involves topical medications in the form of creams, dips, shampoos, and oral medications. With sarcoptic mange, you also have to treat the environment, including washing all bedding and treating the furniture and carpet. Treatment for sarcoptic mange can take a very long time to be successful.

Ringworm

Ringworm is not actually a worm, it is a fungus known as dermatophytes. Ringworm may be passed between humans, dogs, and even cats through direct contact. Puppies are especially susceptible because their immune systems have not yet fully developed. Older dogs and dogs with compromised immune systems are also more susceptible.

Usually, a dog with ringworm will have one or more round, hairless lesions that may also be red and irritated. The round or ring-like shape of the lesions is how this fungus got its name. Typically, these lesions can be seen on a dog's face, ears, and feet.

Your veterinarian can confirm the presence of ringworm through a fungal culture by scraping a bit of skin off of the lesion, preparing a slide, adding some stain, and then looking at the slide under a microscope. Detection can also be through the use of a special ultraviolet light. It is important for the veterinarian to rule out similar-looking dermatological conditions, such as mange.

Puppies are especially susceptible to ringworm.

Ticks can transmit life-threatening diseases.

The treatment for ringworm is an oral anti-fungal medication, which itself may produce serious side effects. Alternatively, the dog can be dipped in lime sulfur, which could discolor your dog's coat and should be done only by the veterinarian. A clean yard is very helpful in reducing further contamination.

Ticks

There are many species of ticks; all of them can dig into a dog's skin and suck his blood. In addition to being entirely disgusting, ticks can transmit some extremely serious, even life-threatening diseases. Ticks are most likely to be found in tall grass, fields, forests, and woods. In certain parts of the country, ticks are more prevalent during the late summer and fall.

Three of the most serious diseases transmitted by ticks are Rocky Mountain spotted fever, Lyme disease, and ehrlichiosis. Lyme disease is caused when a tick infected with the bacterium *Borrelia burgdorferi* bites a dog (or a human). Once infected, a dog may be lethargic, have a fever, or may even limp slightly. Over time, an infected dog becomes anemic. Ehrlichiosis is another tick-borne bacterial infection that affects the blood. Rocky Mountain spotted fever is caused by ticks infected with the *Rickettsia rickettsii* bacterium. In addition to the symptoms described for Lyme disease and ehrlichiosis, dogs with Rocky Mountain spotted fever can have bloody urine, swollen limbs, and bruised skin. All these diseases can be fatal.

Your veterinarian can do a blood test to determine if your dog has a tick-borne disease. Treatment may include certain antibiotics or even steroids. Antibiotics make the bacteria that cause Lyme disease become dormant; they do not kill the bacteria. Dogs who have had tick-borne illnesses may be more susceptible to developing arthritis at an earlier age than normal and with greater severity.

The best course of action is prevention. Some of the flea-prevention topical medications also prevent ticks. While these topicals need to be applied only every one to three months to prevent fleas, they must be used once a month to prevent ticks. In addition, you should check your dog for the presence of ticks on a regular basis and certainly after being in fields or forests. As discussed in Chapter 3, there is a course of Lyme disease vaccinations available, although these vaccinations are not recommended by all veterinarians.

AUSTRALIAN SHEPHERD–SPECIFIC HEALTH ISSUES

While considered to be a generally healthy breed, there are certain diseases and conditions that Australian Shepherds may develop, including epilepsy, hemangiosarcoma, hip dysplasia, hypothyroidism, juvenile cataracts, and lymphosarcoma.

Epilepsy

Epilepsy is an extremely serious, even fatal disease that can be inherited in Australian Shepherds. Dogs with epilepsy have seizures ranging from mild to severe. When a dog has a seizure, he has no control over his movements and may become unconscious; he may even foam at the mouth. This disease is not well understood. It is not always known what brings on a seizure, but there are several possibilities. Causes may include extreme noise such as a severe thunderstorm, blinking lights, or just being overly stressed. Others theorize that there can be environmental triggers, such as the chemicals used to maintain lawns.

It is important to note that some dogs may have seizures but not have true epilepsy. For example, dogs may have seizures because of hypoglycemia, poisoning, heat stroke, or exposure to certain toxic chemicals, such as those used on some lawns. In any event, it should be obvious that you need to take your dog to a veterinarian if he has a seizure.

However, allow the dog to come out of his seizure before moving him. Since he cannot control his movements, he may inadvertently bite you.

The medication used to treat epilepsy is powerful and can have negative side effects. Some dogs with only occasional seizures may not require any medication. If your dog has seizures on a more regular and severe basis, you should discuss this problem with your veterinarian. She can prescribe helpful medications, which may include potassium bromide. Since potassium bromide is toxic in high doses, your veterinarian must continually test the levels of this drug in your dog. Also, you should avoid over-stressing a dog with epilepsy. Epilepsy can never be cured, but in most cases, it can be managed.

Hemangiosarcoma

Hemangiosarcoma, a type of blood cancer, is another disease possible in Australian Shepherds. It may or may not be inherited. It is a terrible, incurable disease that generally occurs in middle-aged and older dogs. This extremely aggressive blood cancer quickly spreads through the blood into the dog's entire body. Often the spleen develops tumors first. There is little or no warning signs with this disease. In the morning, your dog appears to be fine; by that evening, he may collapse due to extensive internal bleeding (mostly likely from a rupture in the tumor). The tragedy of hemangiosarcoma is that by the time you realize your dog has this cancer, it is almost always too late. The kindest thing to do for these dogs is to gently send them into the next world.

Hip Dysplasia

Another potential inherited condition for Australian Shepherds is hip dysplasia, although some experts now maintain that there is an environmental component to this problem as well. A dog's hip consists of a ball-and-socket joint. In dogs with hip dysplasia, the ball or the socket is not properly formed, so that there is not a tight fit between them.

Dogs with severe hip dysplasia may exhibit signs when young. They may be reluctant to go up or down stairs or may even have a slight limp in one or both of their rear legs. They may walk stiffly or have difficulty getting up or lying down. Some believe that raising puppies and dogs on floors that are not slippery will minimize the predisposition toward developing this condition.

If you suspect that your dog may have hip dysplasia, your veterinarian will take an X-ray to examine the formation of your dog's hips while he is under anesthesia, or she may refer you to a specialist. In fact, reputable breeders always check their dog's hips at the age of two years to obtain a hip clearance. Prior to the age of two years, a specialist can do a preliminary examination of a dog's hips, which will disclose the presence of hip dysplasia.

Several surgical options are available to dogs with hip dysplasia, including a total hip replacement, which not only is expensive but requires extensive postoperative care and rehabilitation. Dogs under ten months of age may be candidates for a triple pelvic osteotomy, which involves breaking the hip joint and then reforming it. For less severe cases, your veterinarian may suggest that you manage your dog's condition by making sure he is at his proper weight, putting less strain on his hip joints. Daily exercise to build up the muscles surrounding the hip joint may also be recommended, as this can help keep the joint in place.

There are certain supplements and vitamins that are purported to help dogs with hip dysplasia, including vitamin C, glucosamine, and chondroitin. Often, dogs with hip dysplasia develop early-onset arthritis, which can be extremely painful. For more serious cases, your veterinarian may also suggest certain medications to help control the pain.

Hypothyroidism

Hypothyroidism is a problem where the thyroid gland is not producing enough thyroid hormones. This can also be an inherited disease of Australian Shepherds and is generally found in middle-aged dogs. However, severe cases are detected in young dogs. It is helpful to get a baseline thyroid at 2 years

There are surgical options available to dogs with hip dysplasia.

Keeping a low thyroid dog healthy is easy to manage and inexpensive.

of age. Dogs with low thyroid can become lethargic, lose weight, lose hair, and in more serious cases become aggressive.

If you suspect that your dog has hypothyroidism, take your dog to the veterinarian for a thyroid function test. Your dog's blood sample will be analyzed for various hormones produced by the thyroid gland, including T3, T4, and TSH levels. There is currently tremendous controversy over what constitutes the "normal" range of these hormone levels in dogs. Many experts believe that the current range should be narrowed significantly, which would then mean that more dogs would be classified with low thyroid function.

The treatment for low thyroid is to administer a thyroid replacement pill twice a day, 12 hours apart. In addition, you should have your dog's thyroid function retested about six weeks after he starts using thyroid medication and then about every six months thereafter. Determining the appropriate dose of thyroid-replacement medication can take time and is difficult, but the treatment itself is relatively simple. As a dog ages, his thyroid function will normally decrease, so it is especially important to monitor his thyroid levels during this time. Although hypothyroidism is not curable, keeping a low thyroid dog healthy is easy to manage and inexpensive.

Juvenile Cataracts

Some Australian Shepherds may develop juvenile cataracts, which is opacity of the optic lens. Juvenile cataracts occur in young dogs and are an inherited condition. Dogs who develop cataracts after the age of eight or so years are considered to have cataracts due to aging. During your dog's annual examination, your veterinarian will turn off the lights, put a special instrument over his eyes, and look into his eyes to detect the presence of cataracts. To the naked eye, an eye that appears cloudy or bluish may have cataracts.

If your veterinarian suspects cataracts, she will refer you to a canine ophthalmologist, who can perform more-extensive tests. Some dogs with cataracts progress rapidly into limited vision or even blindness, so it is imperative to consult an ophthalmologist as soon as possible. The ophthalmologist will examine the eye lens using special equipment to magnify the eye and may also perform an eye pressure test. Other diagnostic tests may include electroretinography and ultrasound.

There are several treatments available for juvenile cataracts. These include special eye drops that contain N-acetylcarnosine, which may even improve the dog's eyesight. In extreme cases, the canine ophthalmologist may remove the cataract by performing surgery or may remove the lens and implant a plastic lens. After either of these operations, the dog needs to have special eye drops applied.

Lymphosarcoma

Another cancer that middle-aged Australian Shepherds may get is lymphosarcoma, an aggressive cancer of the lymphatic system that quickly spreads though the dog's entire body. Like hemangiosarcoma, it is incurable, but because signs may be noted earlier in the disease, it may be partially managed. Signs of lymphosarcoma include tumors in the dog's lymph glands, which produces swelling around the throat and perhaps even the feet, and lethargy—dogs with this cancer do not move well, if at all.

The presence of lymphosarcoma can be confirmed by biopsies of the lymph nodes and testing of the dog's bone marrow. Dogs with lymphosarcoma who go untreated generally die within months. In some cases, extensive chemotherapy may prolong a dog's life for about a year. However, the chemotherapy itself can take three or four months. In all cases, even with chemotherapy, the lymphosarcoma will come back, and at that point, there is no further hope. As with hemangiosarcoma, dogs with lymphosarcoma are often put to sleep to avoid further suffering.

GENERAL HEALTH ISSUES

There are certain general health issues that any breed of dog may develop. These issues include certain allergies, ear infections, and eye infections.

Allergies

Allergies are the result of an overactive immune system. Allergies can be caused by food, the environment, or fleas. Symptoms can range from mild to severe.

Dogs who have an allergic reaction to their food often itch excessively. If you suspect that your Aussie may be allergic to something in

Training Tidbit

Some dogs do not like taking pills. To make giving a pill easier, try surrounding the pill in peanut butter or cream cheese. Chances are, your dog will wolf down the peanut butter or cream cheese with the pill inside and never even notice it.

his food, you can try switching to another food with a different protein source. Thanks to the dazzling array of available foods, you can find proteins derived from bison, duck, or salmon. Surprisingly enough, many dogs with food allergies are reacting to the rice commonly found in commercial dog foods, so also look for a food with a different grain source. You can give each food a try and see if your Aussie stops itching.

Some dogs are allergic to certain things in their environment and develop inhalant allergies. One example is leaf mold allergies. Dogs with this problem often scratch compulsively during the fall when so many leaves are on the ground. In cases like this, it is helpful to be diligent in removing the allergen from the environment, if possible. For inhalant allergies, your veterinarian can give your dog antihistamines and, if he has bloodied his skin, cortisone. Bathing your dog in soothing, oatmeal-based shampoos may help stop his itching.

Allergies can be caused by food, the environment, or fleas.

Other dogs are allergic to flea bites, meaning that they are allergic to the fleas' saliva. These dogs will scratch a lot, so flea control is especially important for them. As with environmental allergies, dogs with flea allergies can be treated with antihistamines in combination with cortisone and oatmeal baths.

Allergies should not be confused with just plain boredom or anxiety. Some dogs will lick or bite the hair on their front legs because they are bored or anxious, especially when left alone in the house. They may even bite the hair on their front legs in rows like a corncob. If this is a problem with your dog, you can try leaving him with something to keep him occupied, such as a safe Nylabone stuffed with peanut butter; however, he may need help from a behaviorist. First, however, remember that environmental enrichment, exercise, and interesting toys can go a long way toward preventing this unwanted behavior. Also, allergies should not be mistaken for hypothyroidism, which is easily ruled out by a blood test, as detailed in the previous section.

Ear Infections

The most likely cause of ear infections is canine ear mites (*Otodectes cynotis*). Mites are extremely small insects (related to spiders) that live in a dog's ear canal and can also be present around an infected dog's ears and head. They are extremely contagious to other dogs and cats. They are also irritating. Dogs with ear mites constantly scratch their ears and shake their head. In fact, an infected dog can actually scratch his ears so much that they bleed and lose the surrounding hair. Over time, you may see a thick brown or black substance inside the ear or discharged from the ear. You may even smell a bad odor coming from the ears. In severe untreated cases, dogs can suffer hearing loss that may be permanent.

> # Organic Does Not Necessarily Mean Healthy
>
> Just because something is labeled "organic" does not mean that the substance is not harmful; arsenic is both organic and deadly.

Ear mites are cured through a medication containing insecticide, which is available from a veterinarian. The treatment can take about a month. Because ear mites are so contagious to other dogs and cats, you may also want to treat all the pets in your household. After the dog is free from ear mites, you can use a small amount of olive oil on a cotton ball to keep his ears clean.

Eye Infections

Eye infections can have different causes. The most common are bacteria, irritation, and allergic reactions. A dog with an infected eye may have a green or yellow discharge. His eyes may be red or bloodshot. He may squint. The sand in the corner of his eyes may be excessive and also contain a thick green or yellow discharge. It is important to go to the veterinarian quickly, as dogs may start to scratch or paw at their eyes and damage them.

After ruling out cataracts, your veterinarian will probably prescribe antibiotics in the form of eye drops or eye cream. If the eye infection is the result of an allergy, your veterinarian will help you determine what substance is causing the allergy.

ALTERNATIVE THERAPIES

Alternative therapies in veterinary medicine are becoming more popular. Some traditional practitioners are adding alternative therapies like acupuncture, chiropractic, herbal, homeopathy, physical therapy, and TTouch to their repertoire. Anyone who practices alternative therapies should be appropriately licensed; it might also be preferable to consult a veterinarian who specializes in one of these therapies rather than a nonveterinarian who is licensed in the particular therapy. Before undertaking any of these alternatives, it is prudent to have your veterinarian conduct a thorough physical examination of your dog, including a full blood panel and urinalysis.

Acupuncture

The ancient Chinese healing art of acupuncture is now recognized by many as a viable alternative therapy. Tiny sterilized needles are placed into certain points of the skin to stimulate specific pathways, or meridians, of the body's energy. By so doing, energy is unblocked and able to better flow through and protect the body. Most dogs do not seem to notice when the needles are lightly inserted into their skin, so acupuncture appears to be a painless procedure. Acupuncture is often used on dogs with a painful injury. Some owners have found it especially helpful for relieving arthritis in their senior dogs. If, after weekly visits for six weeks, you do not see improvement, you may want to consider another alternative therapy. Further information about acupuncture can be found on the website for the American Academy of Veterinary Acupuncture (AAVA) at www.aava.org.

Chiropractic

Chiropractic therapy has enjoyed a recent renaissance among dog fanciers, especially among those whose dogs participate in performance events—which many Aussies do. Chiropractic therapy involves adjustments of a dog's bones and muscles. These adjustments help to realign the dog's bones and help joints to move more freely again (also allowing muscles and nerves to function more properly),

Alternative therapies in veterinary medicine are becoming more popular.

which then helps alleviate any pain or other chronic condition. The adjuster first feels the dog's body to locate any areas producing excess heat, indicating underlying trauma. After the adjustment, often you can feel the excess heat being released from the dog's body. Some dogs even shake with relief after their adjustment.

Chiropractic adjustments are especially useful for active dogs, particularly performance dogs, to keep their bodies in maximum condition. It is also useful for dogs who have had injuries and for older dogs afflicted with arthritis. A dog may need an adjustment once a month if he is especially active, but some need adjustments only about once every three months. Many veterinarians who practice chiropractic therapy will show you certain stretching exercises that you can do for your dog before exercising. These exercises help a dog maintain proper alignment. Additional information about chiropractic adjustments can be found on the website for the American Veterinary Chiropractic Association (AVCA) at www.animalchiropractic.org.

Herbal

Herbal therapy involves the use of herbs, applied externally or taken internally, to improve your dog's health. Practitioners of Chinese herbal therapy often use a combination of herbs, as do those who use flower essences for healing. Others prefer to use a specific herb for a particular purpose, for instance to help relax a dog, especially in a stressful situation. There is a popular combination of flower essences used for this very purpose, called Rescue Remedy. Some herbs, such as nettle and licorice root, may be helpful in relieving allergies. Calendula and aloe are used to restore skin health. Other herbs may reduce inflammations. Still other herbs, such as yucca or boswellia, may decrease inflammation and also help with hip dysplasia. And some owners rely on arnica creams to reduce a dog's sore muscles.

Be aware that some herbs may be extremely dangerous, especially in large doses. Therefore, consult your veterinarian before giving your dog any herb. Further information on herbal therapy can be found on the Veterinary Botanical Medical Association (VBMA)'s website at www.vbma.org.

Homeopathy

Homeopathy is based on the theory that "similar cures similar." Essentially, homeopathy practitioners maintain that a very tiny dose of a natural substance, which in large amounts would produce symptoms similar to the target disease, can cure illness. An interesting aspect of homeopathy is that the theory is that the more dilute the substance, the more potent and stronger acting it becomes. There is a lot of controversy over homeopathy, because many who believe in homeopathy do not vaccinate their dogs. Additional information can be found on the American Holistic Veterinary Medical Association (AHVMA)'s website at www. ahvma.org.

Physical Therapy

Physical therapy for dogs relies on many of the same techniques employed in physical therapy for people. The general idea is that these techniques may help the dog move more comfortably. For this reason, physical therapy is often used after a dog sustains a serious injury. In addition, physical therapy can be useful for older dogs who have debilitating arthritis.

Some physical therapy techniques are relatively simple, such as the application of a cold pack or heat, or alternating between the

First-Aid Kit

It is prudent to have an emergency dog first-aid kit located both in your home and in your car. These emergency dog first-aid kits are commercially available. If the kit doesn't include a muzzle, you should purchase that as well. An injured dog is a scared dog. He may not be himself, so you need be very gentle and perhaps even use a muzzle to avoid getting bitten.

two. Other types of physical therapy are more complex, such as electronic stimulation, which involves attaching electrodes to the affected area and then passing a very low-voltage electronic current into the muscle. Other physical therapy techniques employ ultrasonic waves and also water therapy, where dogs swim in specially designed pools under close supervision for short periods of time. This is not a therapy for you to try at home. In some cases, several types of physical therapy are used concurrently.

As with people, physical therapy is not a substitute for medication or surgery. However, it can be helpful when used in conjunction with them and under a veterinarian's supervision.

Tellington Touch

Tellington Touch, also known as TTouch, is a type of therapy created by Linda Tellington-Jones. TTouch is based on the premise that touch is very important to most dogs. TTouch for dogs consists of gentle manipulations of his muscles using your fingers and hands in various positions while using different amounts of pressure. Often, you are supposed to move your fingers and hands in small circular motions on the dog's body. TTouch is used to calm anxious dogs rather than to cure them of physical problems. It is not, strictly speaking, physical therapy. For additional information, go to www.ttouch.com.

EMERGENCY CARE

At the very least, you should know rudimentary emergency care in order to save your dog's life. In particular, you should be able to recognize when to take your dog to an emergency veterinarian (and always know the phone number and location of that clinic). Emergency situations requiring immediate veterinary care include bites and stings (from other dogs and insects), bleeding, broken bones, frostbite, heatstroke, and poisoning. In addition, every pet owner should have a disaster preparedness plan.

Bites and Stings

The two most common types of bites are caused by another dog or a sting from a bee or other insect. If your dog is bitten by another dog, first wash your hands with soap. Then find a clean bandage and wrap the wound. This adds pressure, which helps to stop any bleeding. Your veterinarian will likely give you antibiotics—an ointment to be applied topically and pills to be taken orally. Punctures are never stitched, because they must heal from the inside out. Jagged tears, however, can be stitched.

In the case of stings, try to identify what type of insect stung your dog. Ask your veterinarian in advance for the amount of over-the-counter antihistamine you should give your dog in the event of an insect sting. Often, dogs are stung on their face or inside their mouth, which is especially true of dogs with as much coat as Australian Shepherds. The face will start to swell up quickly and become quite large, which is highly uncomfortable for the dog. If the swelling becomes very pronounced, and especially if the dog's throat starts to close up, race to the veterinarian. Your dog may be having an allergic reaction and probably needs an injection of steroids. In severe cases, the dog will get anaphylactic shock and die. If you know that your dog is allergic to certain insect stings, your veterinarian may give you an Epi-Pen, which contains epinephrine. Even with an Epi-Pen, you still have to get your dog to the veterinarian as soon as possible. Dogs with allergies to insect stings often develop more severe reactions over time.

Bleeding

If you notice any bleeding that cannot be stopped by applying pressure, you need to get your dog to a veterinarian. Rather than removing soaked bandages, keep applying bandages on top of the affected area on your way to the doctor.

Broken Bones

Leg bones are the most likely bone a dog may break. If you think that your dog has a broken leg, wrap his leg in a bandage. In severe cases, you may even see fragments of bone that you will wrap as well. You must take him to the veterinarian immediately.

Frostbite

Frostbite happens when a dog is exposed to subfreezing temperatures for too long and there is localized freezing and damage to certain areas of the skin and tissues. Frostbite usually affects a dog's toes but may also

Frostbite happens when a dog is exposed to subfreezing temperatures for too long.

be found on the ends of his ears. The skin will feel cold and may look very pale. It is important not to use anything warm on the frostbitten area. In such cases, the best thing you can do is take your dog to the veterinarian. If severe enough, the affected area must be amputated. Once an area has gotten excessively cold, it is more likely to become frostbitten upon subsequent exposure to cold. In very cold weather, make sure that your dog has protection, including extra blankets. (Note: Because of their thick double coats, Australian Shepherds do not need clothing to help keep their bodies warm.)

Heatstroke

Heatstroke, a main cause of hyperthermia, occurs when a dog is exposed to excessive heat or dehydration for so long that the body cannot dissipate heat fast enough, and their body temperature rises to a state of emergency. A dog with heatstroke can die very quickly. Dogs can overheat fast because they sweat only from their nose and paws. Sadly, many dogs are left in closed cars during the heat of the summer and then die from heatstroke. The temperature inside a car can, within only minutes, get far higher than the outside temperature. Dogs with heatstroke may not walk very well and can appear drunk. If you think that your dog has heatstroke, put cool water on his face, legs, and belly and then put cool water on the rest of his body. He will need immediate veterinary attention. Dogs who have had heatstroke once are often more prone to getting it again. Always make sure your dog has a supply of fresh water.

Poisoning

Dogs, especially puppies, can easily ingest toxic items. Curiously, certain things are toxic to dogs but not to people, including ethanol (found in alcohol), caffeine, onion (in large amounts), grapes, raisins, chocolate, and xylitol (an artificial sweetener in many sugar-free chewing gums). Even items such as aspirin and ibuprofen can, in sufficient quantities, cause serious damage in a dog. None of these items should be left around the house for your dog to eat accidentally. Two other extremely deadly substances are rat poison and antifreeze, which apparently smells and tastes attractive to a dog.

If you even suspect that your dog has been poisoned, you must immediately call the

In case of emergency, you should have a disaster preparedness plan for yourself and for your dog.

ASPCA Animal Poison Control Center, at 888-426-4435. There is a fee for their services, but their advice could save your dog's life. They will first ask if you know what your dog accidentally ate, so try to ascertain that before calling. They may then direct you to induce vomiting (and they can tell you what to use and how much to use for this purpose) or sometimes specifically not to induce it.

DISASTER PREPAREDNESS

In the aftermath of the nightmare of 9-11, you should have a disaster preparedness plan for yourself and for your dog, especially if you live in one of the targeted urban areas such as New York City or the greater Metropolitan-Washington, DC, area. If you work away from home, find someone close to your home who can take care of your dog in the event that your office undergoes lockdown or if the roads are blocked and you cannot get home. You should make a list of your dog's needs, including what food he eats and the amount and location of the food; any medications your dog takes, including the amount and time given; the name and phone number of your veterinarian; and any special directions. Also indicate where you keep the leashes and any other supplies. Then give that list to your friend along with a key to your house. You can also let your veterinarian know that your friend will be in charge of your dog in the event of a disaster and authorize any fees that may then be incurred. It is also prudent to have your friend visit your dog so that he is familiar with her and will accept being cared for by her.

Multi-Dog Tip

If you have more than one dog, always give each dog his own pills individually and by hand. If you simply put a dog's medication in his food bowl, it is possible that one of your other dogs will race over and eat that dog's food and pill. By giving each dog his own medication by hand, you will be sure that the right dog receives the correct medication.

You should also be prepared for a weather disaster, such as a blizzard or violent windstorm, since either can result in a prolonged loss of electrical power. Make sure that you always have enough extra food to last at least two weeks. You may also want to store extra bottled water to last for two weeks as well. If any of your dogs are on medication, you need at least a two-week supply. If you lose power during the winter in a cold part of the country, you'll need to have extra blankets on hand. If the snow is deep enough, you may have to shovel a pathway in your back yard to allow your dog to be able to relieve himself, especially if he is very young or elderly. Make sure that your dog does not stay outside long enough to either pull muscles in deep snow or develop frostbite.

CHAPTER 9

AUSTRALIAN SHEPHERD TRAINING

For dog lovers, there is nothing more enjoyable in the dog world than being in the company of a well-trained dog. A well-trained dog is a pleasure to live with and can be invited just about anywhere—including other people's homes. Because they are highly intelligent, Australian Shepherds love to learn throughout their lifetime and are easily trained. A daily training session of only ten minutes will help to exercise your Aussie's mind, which needs daily exercise as much as his body does.

In Chapter 4, you learned how to teach your puppy the basic obedience commands of *come* (*recall*), *down, sit*, and *walk nicely on a leash*. Be sure your adult Aussie thoroughly understands these basic obedience commands before moving forward, because they are the building blocks for additional obedience.

Once your dog clearly understands the basic obedience commands, you can proceed to teach him intermediate obedience commands, which include *close, heel, stay, down-stay, sit-stay*, and *stand*.

Another command for your dog to learn is *touch*, which can be a great stress reliever and, more important, keeps training fun.

GETTING STARTED

Here are a few tips to help you get started training intermediate obedience commands to your Aussie.

Treats

Have a ready supply of different treats in your pockets. String cheese works particularly well, especially if you cut it crosswise into small circles. Dog cookies are also good, and you can use different kinds for variety. Alternate which pocket you use to pull a treat from, so that your dog does not fixate on only one side of you. You can vary which particular treat you use to keep things interesting for your dog. If he has an especially difficult time with a certain command, use a treat that he thinks is really special.

Another important thing to remember about using treats is

Want to Know More?

For a refresher on basic obedience commands like *come, down, sit*, and *walk nicely on a leash*, see Chapter 4: Training Your Australian Shepherd Puppy.

to always say "good" combined with whatever command you asked your dog before giving him a treat. If, for example, you asked your dog to sit, when he complies, say "good sit," and then treat him. In time, you may not necessarily give him a treat every time he sits, but you will always tell him "good sit."

Equipment

As will be discussed below, gather your flat-buckle collar, a 2-foot (60-cm) training leash, and a 6-foot (2-m) training leash. These items will be your primary training equipment throughout your dog's life.

Distractions and Distance

In general, you should first teach a command while you are close to your dog and there are no distractions. Once he understands the command, then you can add distance. After that, you can add distractions, but you may have to reduce the distance when you first add a

Training equipment should include a flat-buckle collar, a short training leash, and a longer training leash.

distraction. Distractions can include noise from a television or radio, a person walking past your dog, or even a toy just out of his reach.

Release

As a refresher, always release your dog upon completion of the exercise. For example, if your release command is "free," you can say "sit," "good sit" together with a treat, and then "free." The release tells your dog that work is over for now, until you begin again. Young dogs need breaks between working, and the release command is your way of telling the dog it is break time, even if you start working again quickly.

Start and End on a High Note

Start off each session with a command your dog knows well. This will set a positive tone for the rest of the session. Then introduce one new concept for this session. End the session by repeating the command that your dog already knows, so that you end on a high note. Also, try to end your session while your dog still wants to work a little bit more. This way, you won't tire him out or, even worse, bore him, and he will look forward to your next training session.

Tone of Voice

Australian Shepherds are generally soft, sensitive dogs, so be mindful of your tone of voice. Use a happy tone of voice to encourage your dog. When training obedience commands, it is never wise to use an angry voice, because it will cause your dog to stop working, and he may even start to dislike working. Like other herding dogs, Australian Shepherds are particularly sensitive to tone of voice because they are so tuned in to their owner, including their owner's emotional state.
- By the Numbers
- While Australian Shepherds love to learn

throughout their life, you can overdo a training session. Keep your training sessions short and fun. Be sure to stop training when you notice that your dog is getting tired. Better yet, stop training just before your dog gets tired, because then you will leave him wanting more training!

INTERMEDIATE OBEDIENCE COMMANDS

The intermediate obedience commands for an adult build on the basic obedience commands you already taught your puppy. Most Australian Shepherds are quite precocious and may even start to learn these commands while they are still puppies.

Close

Your Aussie should already know his attention command (explained in Chapter 4)—the command you say when you want him to look at you. You say your dog's name followed by a common attention word, such as *look* or *watch*. The *close* command is another command for getting your dog's attention. With the *close* command, you not only ask your dog to pay attention to you, you ask him to pay attention to you in a particular position—typically sitting by your left side. Most people ask their dog to sit when he is in the *heel* position, which basically means that your dog's ear is aligned with the outside pants seam of your left leg and he is sitting straight. Some people use the word *heel* to get a dog into this position. Since you will be using the word *heel* to ask your dog to walk along with you on your left side (which we will discuss below), using *close* to get him into the initial *heel* position avoids any possible confusion.

How to Teach the *Close* Command
- Put your Aussie in a flat-buckle collar.

This dog is gaiting for a conformation show, which is not the same as heeling.

- Use a 2-foot (60-cm) training leash, not a 6-foot (2-m) training leash; this will help your dog understand that you want him to get close to you by keeping him close to you.
- Put a variety treats in your left pocket, including string cheese.
- Hold the leash in your right hand.
- Put a treat in your left hand.
- As your dog learns the concept, you can eventually put the treat into your mouth and then even hide the treat in your mouth. Cheese works well, since most people like the taste of cheese.
- Say "watch" (or "look" if that's the word you use), and when he does, say "good watch," and give him the treat with your left hand.
- Then—and this is the critical point—using another treat, lure your dog into the *heel*

position (where your dog's ear is aligned with the outside pants seam of your left leg and he is sitting straight). You may have to step backward with your left foot and then bring your left foot back up to your right foot. Keep your body straight as turns can obscure the correct position.
- Once your dog is in the *heel* position, tell him to sit.
- As soon as your dog sits in the *heel* position, he has performed a *close* command. Say "good close" and reward him. Make a huge fuss over his big accomplishment.
- Release him.

Heel

The *heel* is the most fundamental command for formal obedience. In fact, in obedience trials, any ties are decided by having both dogs do more heeling. While you may not desire the precise heeling demanded in obedience trials, it's a good idea to teach your dog to be able to loosely heel by your side. Heeling is important for everyday life with dogs, because it allow you to enjoy your walks together. Dogs who pull you down the street, especially in wet, snowy, or icy weather, are not a pleasure to walk. A dog who heels is far more enjoyable. There are also other times when a *heel* is important. In certain crowded situations, you can better control your dog if he is heeling beside you. Some people even ask their dogs to heel when crossing a street to ensure their safety or even when moving between their house and car.

The formal *heel* position requires the dog to be on your left side. The area from his head to his shoulder should align with your left hip. You generally pick one spot between his head and his shoulder, such his ear, and line up that one spot with the center of the seam of your left pants leg. If you are not planning on competing in obedience, you do not need to be so formal, but your dog should stay on your left side and not constantly move forward, backward, or side to side (which can make you trip). When going for walks, you should not *heel* your dog. Walks are times when your dog should be able to relax, smell the roses, and eliminate when necessary. When taking a walk, you will use the *walk nicely on a leash* command. *Heel* is not for relaxing walks. *Heel* is for formal obedience. Remember, too, that in formal obedience, points are deducted from your dog's score for sniffing or eliminating while performing any exercise, including heeling.

How to Teach the *Heel* Command
- Put your dog in a flat-buckle collar.

- Instead of using your 6-foot (2-m) training leash, attach a 2-foot (60-cm) leash. This will give your dog less wiggle room, especially once you start moving together.
- Fill up your left pocket with a variety of treats. Be sure to include prepared pieces of cut string cheese.
- Put the leash into your right hand.
- Put a piece of string cheese into your left hand.
- Ask your dog to "watch," and when he does, say "good watch," and treat him.
- Then ask your dog to get *close*, say "good close," and reward him.
- Now put another piece of string cheese into your left hand just above his mouth and positioned by your left side and say "heel."
- As you take one step forward, you can let your dog nibble the end of the cheese. Use your hand to cover the rest of the cheese.
- When your dog nicely walks next to you, more or less in *heel* position, say "good heel," and give him more cheese.
- If your dog gets ahead of you, use the cheese to lure him back next to you.
- Ask your dog to walk in *heel* position for only one or two steps. Over time, you can gradually increase the number of steps you take, and then eventually you are heeling nicely together.

Stay
The *stay* command is another important intermediate obedience command. The key to this command is that it means "stay until I tell you to move." In other words, when you tell your dog to stay, your dog is expected to remain in whatever position you left him until you release him.

In formal obedience, the *stay* is used in the *sit*, *down*, and *stand* positions. In the initial or novice level, a group of dogs are in a line,

Stay means "stay until I tell you to move."

and your dog must remain in a *sit-stay* for one minute, followed by a *down-stay* for three minutes, while you are across the 30-foot (9-m) ring. In the next level (the open level), dogs perform a three minute *sit-stay* and a five minute *down-stay*, while their owners are out of sight. For both levels, the owners return to their dogs between the *sit* and *down* parts. In your everyday life, you should never leave your dog on an out-of-sight *stay*, but it is helpful to know the standard for competitive obedience. Also, it may be useful to be able to put your dog on a *stay* in one room of your house while you briefly go into another room.

There are different ideas about which commands you should use to teach the *stay* in the *sit*, *down*, or *stand* position. Let's use the *sit* position as an example. Some people, especially competitive obedience trainers, believe that telling the dog to sit implies that the dog should stay in a *sit* position until

given another command. These people tell their dog only to sit and then expect him to stay in a sitting position without being told the additional command of *stay*. Other people think that it is less confusing to the dog to first be told to sit and then be told to stay. These people first say "sit," and then once the dog is sitting, they say "stay." For your purposes, it may be clearer to the dog to use both the *sit* and then the *stay* commands, as will be detailed below.

Down-Stay

Teaching your dog the *down-stay* can be extremely useful. You may be doing something in the house where you do not want your dog to be underfoot. In these cases, putting your dog on a *down-stay* allows him to still be with you but not to interfere with what you are doing. You may also want your dog to be on a *down-stay* when you open the front door—

especially to visitors. This will allow your visitors to come into your house but ensures that your dog will not escape through the door.

While it is comfortable for a dog to remain on a *down-stay* for a little while (more so than on a *sit-stay* or a *stand*), you do not want to ask your dog to keep a *down-stay* for extremely long periods of time.

How to Teach the *Down-Stay* Command

- As always, put your dog in a flat-buckle collar.
- Use the 6-foot (2-m) training leash to teach all *stays*. This will allow you to gradually move farther away from your dog while maintaining control of his position.
- Put treats into your right pocket. Since *stays* are difficult for young, active Australian Shepherds, you may want to use a really special treat, such as a piece of chicken or an especially favored cookie.
- Hold the leash in your left hand.
- Place a few treats into your mouth. You will not ask your dog to "watch" on a *stay*, because you may want him to remain in

that position for a while—unlike most other commands. If you keep treats in your mouth, he will watch you anyway without being asked.

- Standing beside your dog, ask him to down, say "good down," and reward him. If necessary, put a treat into your hand, lower your hand to the ground, and reward the dog when he does a *down*. As your dog progresses, keep the treat in your mouth and reward him only upon completion of going down.
- While still standing next to your dog, open your right hand to show your flat palm with your fingers together, and then move your palm down in front of—but not touching—his nose while you say "stay."
- Now stand up straight.
- Put the leash into your right hand. Grab a treat in your left hand.
- Say "good down-stay," and give your dog a treat from your left hand. Be sure to give your dog the treat down by his head so that he does not sit up to get the food. You want to reinforce his good behavior in the appropriate down position.
- The concept of a *down-stay* can be difficult, so ask your dog to do a *down-stay* for only a second or two. You can slowly increase the amount of time that he does a *down-stay*.
- If your dog breaks the *down-stay* position, gently but firmly ask him to do another one. Do not reward him for breaking his *down-stay*.
- Once your dog can successfully do a *down-stay* for three minutes with you beside him, ask him to do a *down-stay* and then slowly step directly in front of him with your knees in front of his nose.
- Since this is a new position, ask your dog to remain in a *down-stay* for only a second or two. Over time, you can increase this *down-

stay in the new position to three minutes.

- Now you can slowly add distractions. It is preferable to introduce distractions while you are still next to your dog, because it is easier to help him get back into the desired position when you are next to him.
- The next step is to gradually increase the distance between you and your dog. Do this with you facing him and eventually with you walking around the room. All this is done very slowly in tiny steps.
- Next, you can add distractions together with distance. However, you may have to move closer to your dog again until he understands, and then add distance.

Sit-Stay

The *sit-stay* is another useful command to teach your dog. The *sit* is not as comfortable a position for most dogs as the *down*, so you do not want to ask your dog to remain in a *sit* for long periods of time. However, for short periods of time, it may be ideal. For example, some people ask their dog to do a *sit-stay* before giving them a bowl of food. Others ask their dog to do a *sit-stay* when putting on or taking off their leash, when leaving the house, or when getting in and out of a car. Australian Shepherds can be exuberant, so asking a young Aussie to do a *sit-stay* when greeting people can also be useful.

How to Teach the *Sit-Stay* Command

- Put your dog in a flat-buckle collar, and use the 6-foot (2-m) training leash. This way, you will be able to slowly move farther away

Don't ask your dog to remain in a *sit-stay* for too long.

The *stand* is used in conformation and obedience.

from your dog but still be in control of his position.

- Put treats into your right pocket; use special treats your dog loves.
- Put the leash into your left hand.
- Stuff a few treats into your mouth. Remember that you will not ask your dog to "watch" on a *stay*.
- Standing beside your dog, ask him to sit, say "good sit," and reward him.
- While still standing next to your dog, open your right hand to show your flat palm with your fingers together, and then move your palm down in front of but not touching his nose while you say "stay."
- Stand up straight.
- Put the leash into your right hand and a treat into your left hand.

- Say "good sit-stay," and give your dog a treat from your left hand.
- *Sit-stays* are hard for a dog to understand, so ask your dog to do a *sit-stay* for only one or two seconds. Gradually increase the amount of time for his *sit-stay*.
- If your dog breaks out of the *sit-stay* position, gently but firmly ask him to do another one, and do not reward him for breaking his *sit-stay*.
- After your dog comfortably performs a *sit-stay* for three minutes with you beside him, put him on a *sit-stay* and slowly step directly in front of him with your knees in front of his nose.
- Remember, as with all new positions, to ask your dog to remain in a *sit-stay* for no more than one or two seconds. You can then

gradually increase this *sit-stay* in the new position to three minutes.

- Next, you can gradually introduce distractions, but remember to do so while you are still close to your dog so you are ready to help him get back into the desired position if he breaks it.
- Now, as with the *down-stay*, slowly introduce more distance between you and your dog with you facing him. Eventually, you can walk around the room.
- Later, you can introduce distractions at a distance. Remember that distractions are hard, so you might need to move closer to your dog again until he understands.

Stand

The *stand* is a useful command that you can ask your dog to do while you are grooming or bathing him. You can also ask him to stand when he visits the veterinarian, so that he can be easily examined. Many people ask their dogs to stand when coming into the house so that they can wipe off wet or muddy feet.

How to Teach the *Stand* Command

- Put your dog in a flat-buckle collar, and use the 6-foot (2-m) training lead so you can better control his position.
- Put treats into your mouth; use one of your dog's favorites.
- Put the leash into your left hand.
- Do not ask your dog to "watch," since this is a *stay*.
- Stand beside your dog, and this time, you will face him
- Slowly, move the treat away from his nose but on the same level as his nose, so that in order to get the treat, the dog will step forward into a *stand*.
- Once your dog is in a *stand* position, open your right hand to show your flat palm with

your fingers together, and then move your palm down in front of but not touching his nose, and say "stay."

- At the same time, put your left hand in front of his rear legs and directly under his stomach. This will help to keep your dog in a standing position.
- Stand up straight.
- Say "good *stand-stay*," and give your dog a treat from your right hand.
- As with the *down-stay* and the *sit-stay*, ask your dog to do a *stand-stay* for only one or two seconds. Then slowly increase the amount of time.

Stand can be useful for grooming your Aussie.

- Remember that if your dog breaks out of the *stand-stay* position, gently but firmly ask him to do another one, and do not reward him for breaking his *stand-stay*.
- After your dog comfortably performs a *stand-stay* for a few seconds with you beside him, ask him to do another *stand-stay*, and this time, slowly step directly in front of him with your knees in front of his nose.
- Ask your dog to do a *stand-stay* for only a few seconds. Over time, you can gradually increase up to a few more seconds.
- Generally speaking, your dog will always do a *stand-stay* with you close by, so you do not need to introduce much distance or many distractions.

Touch

The *touch* command is a highly motivating, fun command for your dog to learn. Asking your dog to touch can motivate him in between learning the more formal intermediate obedience commands. If you feel that your dog is stressed, asking him to touch can help relieve his stress and get him focused back onto you and learning. The general idea of this command is that your dog will touch your hand, which is usually held with your palm flat, fingers together, and facing horizontal to the floor.

How to Teach the *Touch* Command
- Use a flat-buckle collar and the 6-foot (2-m) training lead.
- Put treats into your left hand. If you use a piece of string cheese, hide most of the cheese under your thumb, but allow your dog to see the end of the cheese protruding out from under your thumb.
- Put the leash into your right hand.
- Your dog can be in a *sit* or a *stand* next to you. Stand beside him more or less in *heel* position. (This is not a formal obedience command, so your positions do not have to be as precise.)
- Move your left hand just above his nose. Make sure that your dog notices the cheese.
- As your dog moves toward your hand to get the treat, say "touch," "good touch," and allow your dog to have the end of the piece of cheese.
- Over time, you can hold your hand farther away from the dog's mouth. Many Australian Shepherds enjoy jumping up a foot or two (30 to 61 cm) to touch.
- Eventually, you will not need to have food in your hand at all, but remember to always keep some food handy to reinforce your dog's touch from time to time.
- Multi-Dog Tip
- Once your dogs have mastered the *sit-stay* and *down-stay* commands, you can ask them to do their *stays* together. Place your dogs facing in the same direction a few feet apart from each other. Ask any of the better-trained dogs to sit-stay or down-stay first, and then ask your newly trained dogs to do the same. Once they are proficient, you can ask one or more to *sit-stay* and one or more to *down-stay* at the same time.

CHAPTER 10

AUSTRALIAN SHEPHERD PROBLEM BEHAVIORS

At some point in their life, most dogs—including Australian Shepherds—exhibit a few problem behaviors. The cardinal rule is to immediately stop or, better yet, prevent any of these unwanted behaviors before they become a habit. You do not want your dog to learn that doing any of these behaviors is acceptable.

There are several common causes of problem behaviors, which will be covered in detail below.

- First, ask your veterinarian to rule out any physical issues.
- A common cause of problems, especially for active dogs like Australian Shepherds, is not getting enough exercise or training. These dogs are not tired, either physically or mentally, and they need to be both. If they don't get a lot of exercise or training, these dogs end up being just plain bored.
- Some bad behaviors are self-rewarding; the dog simply has fun doing them.
- A few of the more difficult problems to resolve occur because a dog is stressed.

The problem behaviors that are addressed in this chapter are aggression, chewing, counter-surfing, digging, jumping up on people, leash pulling, nipping, and separation anxiety. You'll also find out how to find a professional behaviorist.

COMMON CAUSES OF PROBLEM BEHAVIORS

Because Australian Shepherds are active and intelligent, they tend to get into trouble and test your limits from time to time. This is more or less normal behavior and can quickly be extinguished. Puppies are experts at getting into trouble, as are many young adults. However, if your otherwise well-behaved dog suddenly undergoes a drastic personality change, and not for the better, he may have a physical problem. For example, an older dog who would never hurt a flea but who now snaps whenever you touch his rear may have developed painful arthritis. Pain can cause a distinct personality change. Accordingly, if you notice a sudden change in your dog's personality, take him to the veterinarian to rule out any underlying physical condition—especially any that may be painful to him.

One of the most likely reasons that your Australian Shepherd is getting into trouble is because he, quite simply, is bored. You did not

HOW TO FIND A PROFESSIONAL BEHAVIORIST

Remember the cardinal rule that you stop or prevent unwanted behaviors from happening or becoming a habit? The second cardinal rule is that if you cannot stop or prevent these problem behaviors from occurring, then you must admit that your dog has a problem and immediately seek professional help to fix the problem. In the case of aggression or nipping, you should immediately seek professional help. Aggression and nipping are serious behaviors that require professional help to resolve; if you try to fix them by yourself, you and others are likely to get bitten and hurt.

By this point as a dog owner, you have already found a veterinarian and a training center that you like. The good news is that your veterinarian and the people at your training club, such as your instructor, can quickly direct you to a good professional behaviorist. So finding a behaviorist to help you should simply be a matter of a few phone calls.

After that, you will want to speak with the behaviorist to make sure that you feel comfortable working with her and letting her work with your dog as well. Ask the person if she is familiar with this type of problem and if she has been successful in resolving it. Also ask her how long she has been training dogs, what breeds of dogs she has trained, and if she has accomplished anything in the competitive dog world in obedience events.

Be aware that some people who purport to be professional behaviorists are essentially charlatans. They have no formal training in solving behaviors, problem or otherwise. By relying on the advice of your veterinarian and training club, you will avoid these completely unprofessional people who tend to cause more harm than good.

If you are not providing your Aussie with sufficient daily exercise, he may develop a problem behaviors.

provide him with sufficient daily exercise—both physical and mental. A tired dog generally does not have the energy or the inclination to get into trouble. This is especially true for younger dogs who have higher energy levels.

Australian Shepherds love to have fun. Some problem behaviors are fun to the dog; they are rewarding in and of themselves and are called *self-rewarding behaviors*. These behaviors are especially difficult to extinguish, because the dog rewards himself every time he does them.

Yet another common cause of problem behaviors is that your dog is stressed out. The problems caused by stress are more difficult to fix. You have to first identify what is causing the stress, and then deal with the dog's reaction to that stressing event.

AGGRESSION

One of the most serious and difficult problem behaviors to resolve is aggression. If you are beginning to experience this problem, you must first take your dog to the veterinarian to rule out physical causes, such as illness, painful joints, hypothyroidism, brain tumors, epilepsy, and other illnesses and diseases.

Aggressive behaviors do not appear instantly, they gradually develop over time. At the first signs of aggression, it is imperative that you consult a professional behaviorist. Signs of aggression may begin as a curled lip, a low rumble in the throat that you can feel only through the leash, a lowered body stance, pinned back or erect ears, or raised hairs on your dog's shoulders, which are called hackles. Do not wait until your dog is leaping about growling and snapping to call for help. The sooner you ask for help, the easier and faster it will be to resolve this problem.

The good news is that true aggression is relatively rare in Australian Shepherds. The bad news, however, is that true aggression is never cured; it is only managed and that management must be done by you to protect both your dog and yourself. In this day and age of extreme liability, it is your responsibility to ensure that your dog does not harm anyone.

Dominance Aggression

There are several different types of aggression. One type of aggression, *dominance aggression*, usually appears around the onset of puberty—between 10 and 18 months, when the dog's hormones begin to kick in to his system. In effect, these dogs are acting like surly teenagers. Dogs with this type of aggression want to assert their superiority and dominance over the other dogs in the household (if there are any), and sometimes even over the people in the household, including perhaps even their owner. They often try to keep the resources they deem important all to themselves. Different resources have varying degrees of importance to a dog, but any resource guarding is a form of dominance aggression. Examples of resources that a dog may guard include food, bones, toys, his bed, your bed or sofa, and especially you. If your dog tries to prevent another dog or a person (including you) from getting access to his resource, he is exhibiting resource guarding. If he tries to take any of these resources from another dog or a person (including you), that is also resource guarding. You should be able to take any resource away from your dog, meaning you should be able to take a toy from him or tell him to get off of your bed without any issues. If you cannot, he is being dominant.

Fear Aggression

A more common type of aggression is *fear aggression*, which occurs in certain social situations where the dog feels so afraid that he becomes aggressive. Early and often, socialization goes a long way toward ensuring that a dog does not become fear aggressive, but even older but poorly socialized dogs can benefit from being socialized. However, many believe that there may be a genetic as well as

By the Numbers

If you got your Australian Shepherd when he was eight weeks old, chances are that he won't develop any of these problem behaviors—because you properly trained and socialized him.

True aggression is rare in Australian Shepherds.

regain order—even if they have to be aggressive.

A very common type of fear aggression happens while on a leash. Remember that Australian Shepherds are extremely sensitive; they will sense your fear and concern traveling down that leash from you to them. These dogs generally start to snap and growl when they see another dog pass close to them as, for example, when you go into and out of your training club. In these cases, make sure that your leash is short so you keep your dog close to you, and above all, keep your leash loose. A tight leash signals to these dogs that you are afraid, so they react by being afraid too. Put your hand under the dog's collar at the top of his neck if you need better control. Of course, in this case, as in all cases of aggression, you need to see a professional behaviorist as soon as possible.

Professional Help

With any aggressive behavior, a professional behaviorist will ask you when the incidents occur and what happened. By asking these questions, she is trying to identify what exactly triggers your dog to act aggressively. It can be really helpful to keep a journal and write down when your dog was aggressive in order to identify possible triggers for his aggression. You can also record exactly what he did to show his aggression to determine the severity of his response.

CHEWING

All dogs chew—it is a normal and natural behavior for them. Chewing is in itself rewarding, so dogs love it. However, some dogs chew inappropriately. Problem chewing almost always goes back to the owner for not preventing it in the first place.

You puppy-proofed your home and yard for your puppy. This may need to be a life-long situation in that you may never be able to leave

environmental component to fear aggression.

Fear aggression is expressed in social situations that the dog finds frightening. For example, your dog may be afraid of someone else touching him, such as your veterinarian or groomer. He may be afraid of small children who are running and screaming. He may be afraid of other dogs, especially dogs who are out of control and are barking and leaping about while on leash. As herding dogs, Australian Shepherds like to be in control; they love order. They may view these disruptive small children and dogs as being out of control and mistakenly believe that it is their job to certain highly desirable and chewable items around your home or yard. Some people need to keep their shoes and slippers in their closets for the life of their dog. Some dogs like to chew pockets out of pants that contained treats, so these owners need to keep their pants in their closets as well.

As with any problem behavior, you need to first figure out the motivation or trigger. Generally speaking, dogs chew when they are bored. This is especially true for active and intelligent dogs like Australian Shepherds. Daily walks and tennis-ball-throwing sessions in your back yard will tire him out physically, and daily (but short) training sessions will tire him out mentally. Your Aussie needs to be completely tired, both physically and mentally.

Puppies go through periods of teething during which chewing relieves the pain of their erupting teeth. Also, teething puppies need to chew to help their teeth break through their gums. These teething puppies need a steady supply of items to chew. Some companies, including Nylabone, make puppy teething toys that have the necessary hardness for their teething but are safe for them to chew.

Some dogs chew because they are anxious about being in a crate, which is especially true of older dogs who may have been rescues. These dogs have never been trained to be in a crate, so you need to start at the beginning and crate train them as you would a puppy. Other dogs chew due to anxiety about being left alone; separation anxiety will be discussed later in this chapter.

Prevention and Solutions

As with other problem behaviors, the key to stopping destructive or inappropriate chewing is to prevent it in the first place. If your dog chews something he should not be chewing, you must never let it become a habit.

Some objects, however, cannot be put away in closets or drawers. All puppies love to unroll toilet paper. To prevent a toilet-papered house, simply close the bathroom door. Most dogs love to empty trash, so you need to use trashcans with lids and keep them under the sink or somewhere out of reach. Use common sense to prevent your dog from getting to objects he wants to chew but that he shouldn't, and this will prevent most chewing issues in the first place.

No puppy or adult should be given the run of the house—even with you present—until he has earned that privilege. You must also watch and supervise his behavior until you are convinced that he can and will roam the house safely and without destroying anything, especially when you are not there. You can start by keeping him in whatever room you are in,

Daily physical exercise can help with a problem chewer.

so that you can supervise him. Baby gates are helpful for limiting his access to the rest of the house. In time, you can grant him access to another room, and so on, until he has the run of the house while you are present.

Give him appropriate toys to play with and chew, such as Nylabones. You can keep toys in a laundry basket and allow him to select the ones he wants to play with or offer him some toys yourself. Since inappropriate objects like shoes and slippers are safely put away out of his reach in your closet, he will not be able to chew them. If you cannot closely supervise your dog, put him into his crate with a special toy to occupy him.

If you forgot and left something very exciting out that your dog is now chewing, then you need to do something immediately. Grab a really favored toy, wiggle it around a bit to get his attention, and tell him "no chew." Chances are that your dog will immediately drop whatever he is chewing and reach for his favorite toy instead. Tell him "good," and quickly put the other object out of his reach (which you should have done in the first place!).

Many Australian Shepherds mature mentally at around the age of three years. You probably do not want him to roam the house alone when you are away until he reaches this age. Even so, you need to permit him access to your house step by step. Start by leaving him in your bedroom, which may already contain his crate. Leave him special toys and treats that he gets only when you are gone. Leave him alone

for just a few minutes, then return. You can gradually increase the time you leave him alone in your room. If he begins to chew something inappropriate, such as your pillows, then it is too early to leave him loose in your bedroom. Put him into his crate while you are away.

However, if after a few weeks, he seems responsible enough to be loose in your bedroom, then you can try giving him access to another room in your house, while putting up baby gates to prevent him from going into other areas of your house. Again, leave for only a few minutes, and then return to make sure he has behaved. If you return to find him chewing your sofa pillow, then he needs to go back to your bedroom or into his crate when you leave the house.

COUNTER-SURFING

Counter-surfing is perhaps the ultimate self-rewarding behavior. The dog puts his front feet on the counter, sniffs around until he finds some food on the counter, and then grabs and eats the food. Australian Shepherds are notorious for being avid counter-surfers.

Prevention

There really is no reliable method of training a dog not to counter-surf, especially one who has already tasted the delightful results of a counter-surfing foray. As such, it is up to you to never leave any food out on any kitchen counters. By logical extension, you must never leave any food within your dog's reach, and this

Give your dog safe chews to help prevent inappropriate chewing.

includes kitchen and dining room tables as well as coffee tables. Many a motivated Aussie has been known to leap onto the kitchen counter or dining room table, and coffee tables go without saying. Being excellent and enthusiastic jumpers, you may be surprised at your adult Australian Shepherd's reach, especially when motivated by the presence of food.

Want to Know More?

For a crate-training refresher, see Chapter 4: Training Your Australian Shepherd Puppy.

DIGGING

Digging is another self-rewarding behavior to dogs. Some dogs simply love to dig. You have already puppy-proofed your yard, but you do not want to see a crater in the middle of your lawn.

Prevention and Solutions

As with any problem behavior, the key is to prevent your dog from digging in the first place. To do so, you first need to figure out why your dog is digging. A common reason for digging is that your dog is just terribly bored. Another reason may be because your dog is too hot and needs to cool off in the cooler ground. Pregnant dogs often dig right before or after they have puppies, because they want to hide their puppies in the hole for safety. In a few cases, a dog digs to try to escape—this is a type of anxiety disorder.

For bored dogs who elect to dig holes in your yard, you need to provide more stimulation. As always, be sure to tire out your dog every day both physically (with a daily walk and with a round of tennis ball throwing in your yard) and mentally (with a training session). If

Some dogs love to dig.

Dogs who are tired both physically and mentally are less likely to develop problem behaviors. Be sure that you give your dog a daily walk followed by a short training session.

he continues to dig, you may need to increase both types of exercise. Dogs are social animals hard-wired to live in packs. If you have only one dog, getting him a friend to play with will help relieve his boredom. If you do not want to get a second dog, you may want to find a friend with a well-socialized dog and arrange play dates for your dog.

You also need to supervise his time outside. Start by staying outside with him whenever you put him outside. When he begins to dig, say "no dig," and divert his attention elsewhere, perhaps by throwing a tennis ball. Tell him "good no dig" when he stops digging and races for the ball.

As an alternative, some people decide that a hole in one particular part of the yard is preferable to a field of craters all over the yard. They permit their dog to dig but only in that one spot. Every so often, they may need to fill up the hole, and their dog will again begin to dig but only in that one place.

If your dog is digging a hole to cool himself, the hole is likely to be next to your house or under a shrub. Dogs are susceptible to heatstroke, as we discussed in Chapter 8: Australian Shepherd Health and Wellness. No dog should be left outside so long that he becomes overheated in the first place. For these types of diggers, the simple solution is to bring your dog inside, give him some fresh and cool water, and help him to cool down.

Pregnant dogs or those with newborn or very young puppies dig out of maternal instinct. This behavior will quickly extinguish. Further, breeding dogs is a serious endeavor and requires an entire book in and of itself; dog breeding will not be addressed here.

If you find that your dog is digging to escape, then you need to consult a professional behaviorist immediately. A dog who tries to dig out of your yard to escape is suffering from extreme anxiety and needs help. Further, most jurisdictions have leash laws such that loose dogs are illegal and perhaps even a criminal misdemeanor, possibly resulting in a fine or even the removal of your dog. Loose dogs can get hurt or killed by cars. They can get into dog fights or even hurt people, especially young children and people riding bikes. It is imperative that you not allow your dog to dig out from your yard both for his sake and that of the community.

There are extreme measures that you can take to more solidly secure your fencing. A dog who tries to dig out of your yard may soon try to jump out of your yard as well. You can add additional height to your fence with a topper that is about 4 feet (1 m) and angled in toward your yard. You can bury 2 feet (61 cm) or so of wire underneath your fence. But whatever additional fencing you put in place, you need to always be outside with your dog when you let him outside.

JUMPING UP ON PEOPLE

Australian Shepherds love to jump and are marvelous jumpers. They especially love to jump when they are excited and happy, and most Aussies are happy to jump up on people too. Jumping is another natural, self-rewarding behavior and is best handled by prevention in the first place.

If your dog is jumping up, ask for an alternate behavior, like a *sit*.

Prevention and Solutions

An eight-week-old puppy will try to jump up on you. At that point in his life, he will reach only to below your knees. By four months of age, however, he will be able to jump up to your nose, and he will weigh considerably more. Many Australian Shepherds love to try to jump and spring off of people they especially like. If you do not allow your puppy to jump on you, it will go a long way toward stopping your adult from jumping on people as well.

To stop an eight-week-old puppy from jumping, simply turn your back or side to him. He will then be forced to lower his front feet, as they will slide down anyway. For adults who have not been trained, turning your back or side to him may even encourage him to jump. Many Australian Shepherds have a particular fondness for jumping on their owners when their owners have their back to them because they find it amusing.

For adult Australian Shepherds, you need to use another method of preventing him from jumping up on you. Present both of your hands, palm open and up, toward your dog. This gesture generally stops a dog from jumping and, in any event, takes most of the fun out of it for the dog. Say "no jump" when he is about to jump and then "good no jump" when he does not jump or when his four paws are on the floor.

Visitors can be especially exciting and happy events to Australian Shepherds. They just cannot contain themselves and will try to jump up on your guests. If your Aussie is like this, there is a simple solution. Put on his buckle collar and leash, and get some treats for your pocket. Then walk him over to the door. When you are close to the door but far enough away so that the door can open without hitting your dog, ask him to sit and then to sit-stay. Have a treat ready to reward him, and say "good sit-stay." This way, he'll never have the opportunity to jump on your guests, and you have reinforced his good behavior of sitting on command. Your visitor can tell your dog "good sit-stay" and offer him a treat as well.

LEASH PULLING

Leash pulling is another fun, self-rewarding behavior for dogs. While Australian Shepherds are not driven to pull as much as some other breeds, such as Alaskan Malamutes or Siberian Huskies, many an Australian Shepherd enjoys pulling.

You've already taught your puppy to walk nicely on a leash (as explained in Chapter 4: Training Your Australian Shepherd Puppy), and you've taught your adult dog to heel (as detailed in Chapter 9: Australian Shepherd Training). Because of your obedience training, your Aussie should walk comfortably on a leash with you.

Yet certain triggers may cause even a well-behaved dog to start to pull on his leash.

Australian Shepherds can weigh from 40 to 60 pounds (18 to 27 kg), so when they decide to pull, they can bring a person down to the ground.

Prevention and Solutions

If you are enrolled in an obedience class, your instructor can work with you individually to help you correct leash pulling.

In the meantime, be aware that as a herding dog, some sudden movements may overly excite an Australian Shepherd and cause even a well-trained dog to pull on his leash. For example, a jogger, running children, a scampering cat, and of course cars may trigger his herding instinct so that he pulls on his leash. This can happen quite suddenly.

To resolve this issue, be aware of your environment at all times. If you see any of these triggers, be prepared that your dog may suddenly lunge forward. Make sure you always walk your dog on a buckle collar and a 6-foot (2-m) leash. Don't use a retractable leash, because it applies constant pressure to a dog's neck, which may increase their desire to pull. Therefore, retractable leashes can sometimes reinforce and train a dog to pull on lead. Plus, the farther away your dog is on lead, the harder it is for you to control his pulling. For all these reasons, walk your dog on a 6-foot (2-m) leash and not a retractable one.

When your dog pulls on the leash, brace your feet and stop. By stopping, you take a lot of the fun of pulling away from the dog. If you notice that your dog has spotted a trigger, such as a bicyclist, then you may have time to quickly turn and walk away from the trigger. Your dog cannot pull, because he must also turn and walk with you in the opposite direction from the trigger. You can also do a right or left turn—both of which will divert your dog's attention to you and away from what caused him to pull in the first place. With either

method, give your dog a treat when he comes toward you. No dog should heel while on his daily walk, but if he decides to lunge, then after turning, you can ask him to heel for a few quick steps. You can reward him with a "good heel" and a treat, thereby reinforcing the good behavior while ignoring the bad behavior.

NIPPING

Nipping can easily become an out-of-control behavior requiring you to quickly consult with a professional behaviorist. As with any unwanted behavior, the solution depends on the trigger.

Prevention and Solutions

Eight-week-old puppies and puppies who are teething may from time to time nip when they become overly excited playing with you. If your puppy tries to nip your fingers, pull your hand away and loudly and painfully say "ouch." Then stop playing with your puppy. This way, you have taken away his fun. You can even squirt your hand with a commercially available bitter-tasting spray that is distasteful (yet safe) to dogs. If however, he continues to nip, then you need to seek help.

As herding dogs, some older Australian Shepherds may nip as an attempt to control what they perceive as an out-of-control

Multi-Dog Tip

Some dogs learn problem behaviors by watching other dogs. If one of your dogs exhibits any of these problem behaviors, quickly work to stop that behavior before your other dogs start doing it too.

As herding dogs, Aussies may nip as a means of controlling a situation.

situation. They may try to nip small, screaming children who are running around. These dogs should never be left alone with small children, and you need to consult a behaviorist to prevent a child from being hurt.

Another ramification of a herding dog's natural instincts is that certain movements may attract his attention. A bicyclist or jogger may cause your dog to want to contain their movement. He may nip in his attempt to herd them. To prevent this, your dog should always be on leash when you take him out of your house. If you see any bicyclists or joggers, make sure your dog is close enough to you that he cannot possibly get close enough to nip them. This is another situation where you need professional help.

SEPARATION ANXIETY

One of the more serious types of problem behaviors is separation anxiety. Dogs with separation anxiety become extremely destructive when left alone. Even if you have crate trained your puppy, your adult may develop separation anxiety when his hormones kick in. These dogs may become extremely

destructive and chew your sofa, dig by your door, and generally wreak havoc throughout your house. They may also become self-destructive and chew their front legs until they bleed. If your dog is suffering from separation anxiety, he should always be put into a crate when you leave the house. However, before crating him, be sure that you have thoroughly physically and mentally exercised him. Also, turn on the radio in the room where he is crated, and give him something to occupy himself. Plastic toys designed for dogs that can be stuffed with peanut butter can be helpful.

It goes without saying that you need to immediately consult a professional behaviorist to manage your dog's separation anxiety. In extreme cases, after a thorough physical examination, the behaviorist may recommend that you also consult your veterinarian. Certain medications are available that, though powerful, may help calm your dog. The goal is for you to give your dog these calming medications only as needed while your professional behaviorist works with you to help resolve your dog's separation anxiety.

CHAPTER 11

AUSTRALIAN SHEPHERD SPORTS AND ACTIVITIES

The activities that you and your versatile Australian Shepherd can participate in are limited only by your time and imagination. Australian Shepherds can do any sport or activity you ask them to do. They are smart, active, energetic dogs who thrive on learning and doing things with their owner.

ACTIVITIES

You can easily incorporate your well-trained Australian Shepherd into any family activity. These activities may include camping, walking, and jogging. Plus, the American Kennel Club (AKC) has two programs that can help you train and socialize your dog.

Camping

Some, but not all, campgrounds welcome dogs. Be sure to check the rules in advance so you know if you will be allowed to take your dog camping with you. If you do take him, you should keep him on a leash at all times, as the likelihood of even a well-trained dog bolting after a leaping deer or rabbit is high. Always be sure to clean up after your dog. Do not allow him to drink any standing water to avoid possibly obtaining internal parasites. Also, check him for ticks every evening.

Walking and Jogging

When you brought your Australian Shepherd into your home, you incorporated a daily walk with him into your schedule in order to exercise him physically. Jogging, however, should never be done with puppies. You must wait until the dog's growth plates are closed, which occurs at about 18 months, to avoid injuring his legs. Start with short distances and gradually build up your dog's endurance over time. As with camping, remember to clean up after your dog.

The AKC S.T.A.R. Puppy Program

The AKC recently introduced their S.T.A.R. Puppy Program as an effort to motivate owners to take their puppies through a puppy or basic obedience class. "S.T.A.R." stands for "socialization, training, activity, and responsibility." This program is a great way to start your puppy off on the right paw to being trained and socialized. Completion of this program facilitates your dog's success in the AKC's next program, the AKC Canine Good Citizen Program, which will be discussed below. Puppies up to one year of age are eligible for the S.T.A.R. Puppy Program and must complete a six-week class taught by an

AKC-approved evaluator. At the end of the class, the puppy must pass an examination, and the owner must pledge to be a responsible dog owner.

The AKC S.T.A.R. Puppy Program test consists of 20 behaviors, which include certain behaviors from the owner, identified behaviors from the puppy, and pre-Canine Good Citizen behaviors from the puppy. The six owner behaviors deal with responsible dog ownership. The five puppy behaviors concern basic training and socialization. The nine pre-Canine Good Citizen behaviors involve a combination of basic and intermediate obedience commands and additional socialization.

Once you and your puppy have passed the S.T.A.R. Puppy examination, you can then register your puppy with the AKC S.T.A.R.

Puppy Program. The AKC will send you a medal and a certificate. The AKC's website (www.akc.org) has additional information about this program.

The AKC Canine Good Citizen Program

The AKC instituted their Canine Good Citizen Program in 1989 (well before their newer S.T.A.R. Puppy Program), which is designed to help you socialize and train your dog. There is no age limit for this program. Although you do not need to attend a class to take the test, it would certainly help you and your dog to pass the test. To take the test, your dog will have to be on a 6-foot (2-m) training lead, and you'll need to bring his comb or brush to the exam. You must sign a pledge to be a responsible dog owner, and then you and your dog take the

Some campgrounds welcome dogs.

By the Numbers

Australian Shepherds are active, intelligent dogs who are extremely versatile. They can learn to do just about any sport or activity. However, puppies and young dogs should not be jumped until after their growth plates close, which occurs at around 18 months. You can, however, introduce jumping to your dog by asking him to step over a pole set on the ground, known as a ground pole. Once your dog matures, jumping will not be a problem, as Australian Shepherds are natural and excellent jumpers.

test. You can repeat commands and use your voice to motivate your Aussie, but you may not use food or toys as motivators.

The test itself has ten parts. The specific parts of the test are behaving nicely with a stranger; sitting while a stranger pets your dog; looking well groomed and accepting being combed or brushed by you and the examiner; walking nicely on a loose lead while on a walk; walking politely through a crowd of people; responding to the commands , , and ; performing a recall; behaving nicely around another dog; behaving when distracted; and acting calm and polite while with a stranger but without his owner.

After successful completion of the AKC Canine Good Citizen test, you will be mailed a certificate. Best of all, your dog will earn the AKC Canine Good Citizen title, which can be placed after his name as "CGC." The AKC provides more detail about their Canine Good Citizen Program and test on their website at www.akc.org.

SPORTS

The world of competitive sports is wonderful to explore with Australian Shepherds because they truly excel in all of them. Even if you never want to compete with your dog, both of you can greatly enjoy learning and participating in these sports. Some of the sports you might enjoy with your dog include agility, canine freestyle, conformation, herding, and obedience.

Before beginning any sport, have your vet conduct an overall wellness examination of your dog to make sure that he is fit to participate. In particular, you want your dog to be at a good weight.

Agility

Agility is an obstacle course you and your dog must successfully complete within a set time. It is a very fast sport for both dog and handler involving much running, jumping, twisting, and turning.

There are many different agility obstacles, including single-bar to triple-bar jumps, tunnels, weave poles, a tire, a teeter totter, a pause table, a dog walk (which is an elevated platform that your dog must walk onto and off of), and an A-frame (which has a very steep slope up and then down). Some of these obstacles have contact zones requiring that your dog have at least one paw in the zone to qualify.

There are many different agility classes, and more seem to be added all the time. Some involve just jumps and weave poles; others

Agility is a fast-paced, exciting sport.

involve all the obstacles. Within each class, there are different jump heights depending on the height of your dog at the withers. Most Australian Shepherds jump either 16 or 20 inches (41 to 51 cm), but it depends on the individual dog.

Both the AKC and the Australian Shepherd Club of America (ASCA) offer titling events in agility, and Australian Shepherds have been extremely successful agility dogs. Even if you never want to compete, you and your dog may enjoy agility training.

Your dog must be in excellent condition to do agility. If your dog is overweight, you first have to get his weight under control. For older dogs who are still in good shape, there is a preferred class where the jump heights have been lowered.

Canine Freestyle

Canine freestyle, commonly referred to as doggie dancing, involves training your dog to execute choreographed movements with you set to music. There are two main canine freestyle organizations. The Canine Freestyle Federation, Inc. (CFF) was created in 1995 and offers more information on its website, www.canine-freestyle.org. The World Canine Freestyle Organization, Inc. (WCFO) was founded in 2000, and its website is www.worldcaninefreestyle.org. These organizations offer several titles in competitions throughout the United States.

Conformation (Showing)

Almost every puppy owner dreams that her perfect puppy will grow up to be a breed champion. A conformation event (or breed show) is the means to getting your champion. Australian Shepherds may become champions in several venues, typically either the AKC or the ASCA. In these shows, breeds of dogs are judged not against each other but against the breed standard. Each club has a slightly different breed standard, and the basics of each standard were explained in Chapter 1In either venue, your dog must be of sufficient quality in both physical structure and temperament that he merits a breed championship.

Showing a dog in the breed ring requires a lot of preparation. You must first condition your dog. Then you have to train your dog to trot, or gait, and to stand while being physically examined by a judge. For the show itself, you have to extensively groom your Aussie, and you yourself have to be polished and generally presentable. Many people prefer to hire a professional handler so they can enjoy watching their dog being shown. Your breeder or training club can offer suggestions about finding a professional handler whom, of course, you will have to interview. In particular, you will want a detailed explanation of the handler's fees.

In a breed show, each breed is first shown against others of its own breed. The breed is divided so that males show against males, and females show against females. Within this initial division, the show is divided into various classes based on age and color. Through a process of elimination, the best class male is selected by the judge, who declares him to be Winner's Dog. The same is done for the best class female, who becomes the Winner's Bitch. Both the Winner's Dog and Winner's Bitch are awarded points toward their championship based on the number of other class dogs they defeated. Points range from one (in small shows) to five (in large shows). In the AKC, an Australian Shepherd must obtain at least three points in two different shows. In the

Want to Know More?

For more information about the Australian Shepherd's breed standards, go to Chapter 1: Is the Australian Shepherd Right for You?

ASCA, an Australian Shepherd must be awarded three or more points in three different shows. These wins based on three or more points are called majors.

Once the Winner's Dog and Winner's Bitch have been selected, they return to compete in the Best of Breed part of the competition, which includes other finished breed champions. The judge will first decide which winning dog he prefers, the dog or the bitch, and then declare that dog to be the Best of Winners. This dog, the Best of Winners, then

Australian Shepherds may become show champions in several venues, typically either the AKC or the ASCA.

keeps either the originally awarded number of points or that of the other sex, whichever is higher. It is therefore possible for a class dog or bitch to obtain a major by becoming the Best of Winners. Then both winning dogs will compete against the other breed champions. The judge will select both a Best of Breed and a Best of Opposite Sex, who must be the opposite sex of the Best of Breed winner. The Winner's Dog and Winner's Bitch are eligible for consideration for either the Best of Breed or the Best of Opposite Sex. A new title of Grand Champion now is available.

Herding

Many people want to at least try their Australian Shepherds on sheep to see if they have any instinct—after all, they are sheepdogs. Be sure to find a reputable trainer to avoid hurting your dog or yourself. Often, it takes a few times before your dog "turns on" to the sheep and starts working them. Be patient and you may be pleasantly surprised. One of the most beautiful sights in the world is watching your dog rely on his instincts to herd stock. For more-advanced dogs, both the AKC and the ASCA offer herding trials with various levels of competition. Stock includes ducks, sheep, and cattle.

Obedience

Competitive obedience requires consistency and precision by both you and your dog. Many consider obedience to be the ultimate demonstration of teamwork between a dog and his handler. Indeed, watching a well-trained obedience team is a thing of beauty. Australian Shepherds make excellent obedience dogs and enjoy obedience training even if you never want to title them.

For the open level of obedience, your dog must retrieve a dumbbell over the high jump.

Obedience titles can be obtained in both the AKC and the ASCA. There are three general levels of obedience known as novice, open, and utility. Each level requires a dog to qualify three times under two different judges.

At the novice level, you and your dog together must do your individual exercises, which are heel on leash and a figure eight, heel off leash, stand for examination, and recall. After everyone has completed their individual runs, you and your dog will participate in the group exercises consisting of a long sit for one minute followed by a long down for three minutes. Earning the novice title of Companion Dog entitles you to put "CD" after your dog's name.

For the open level, the individual exercises consist of heel off leash, drop on recall, retrieve on the flat (meaning that your dog retrieves a dumbbell after you throw it), retrieve (a dumbbell) over the high jump, and broad jump. The group exercises are a long sit (a three-minute stay with the handler out of sight of the dog) and then a long down (a five-minute down with the handler out of sight of the dog). Obtaining the open title of Companion Dog Excellent allows you to use the initials "CDX" after your dog's name.

The utility level consists entirely of individual exercises, most of which involve hand signals instead of verbal commands. The dog must complete the signal exercise (in which the handler gives signals across the 30-foot [9-m] ring asking the dog to down, sit, and then come), scent discrimination (where the dog must select a scented article out of a pile of eight unscented articles), directed retrieve (in which the dog must retrieve one of three gloves as directed), moving stand and examination (where you and your dog heel, you tell your dog to stand-stay as you move about six steps away from him, the dog remains in a stand

Training Tidbit

Training in more than one sport or activity at a time is called cross-training. Many trainers believe that cross-training actually improves a dog's performance in all venues in which he is being trained and prevents a dog from becoming bored with any one venue.

while the judge examines him, and then you call your dog to heel), and directed jumping (where you send your dog straight out to the end of the ring, ask him to sit, and then ask him to jump either a high jump on one side of the ring or the bar jump on the other side; the dog must do this twice, taking each jump as directed by you). The utility title is called Utility Dog and has the initials "UD."

There are also more and less advanced obedience classes. For a Companion Dog Excellent or "CDX," you and your dog must qualify in an open and a utility class on the same day at the same show and then do so ten times. For the Obedience Trial Champion or "OTCH," your dog must earn points based, in the AKC, on beating other dogs or, in the ASCA, achieving sufficiently high scores.

THERAPY WORK

Therapy work is an excellent activity for you and your Aussie to do together. It is especially good for older dogs who may no longer be able to participate in other sports and activities but still want to be a team with you. A therapy dog must be super-socialized and extremely calm, gentle, and friendly in all situations.

Certain organizations can certify your dog

Your Aussie is too large to fly in the cabin of a plane under your seat.

The element of behaving around distractions is made more difficult, because the dog and handler must walk within three feet of food on the ground. Also, the dog must remain calm when walking around people who are shuffling or limping, or breathing hard or irregularly. Some of these people may be in a wheelchair or using crutches. There is an 11th additional element, which is that your dog must be able to say hello nicely to a person. The dog will also be tested to see if he is calm around children who are actively playing or running.

After passing the TDI test and enrollment in their program, which involves a fee and a medical certification, TDI may, in certain situations, offer you insurance. The TDI enrollment must be renewed on an annual basis.

TRAVEL

A well-socialized, well-trained dog is a great travel companion. You can take such a dog almost anywhere in your car or even by plane. You can safely stay overnight in dog-friendly hotels. However, if you cannot take your dog with you when traveling, you can leave him home with a pet sitter or board him. Whether or not you travel with your dog, you may want to send him to doggy day care.

as a therapy dog. One of the most prominent certifying organizations is Therapy Dogs International, Inc. (TDI). Some of their certification requirements include elements of the AKC's Canine Good Citizenship test (described above), but the certifying entity is TDI, not the AKC. A dog can take just the CGC test, but he may take the TDI test only if he again takes the CGC test at the same time that he takes the TDI test.

The TDI test is designed to show that your dog has sufficient confidence and is under enough control to be qualified to visit hospitals, assisted living facilities, schools, and other such places. The elements of the TDI test include the ten elements of the AKC CGC test.

How to Travel With Your Dog

One thing to remember when traveling with your dog is to always carry a current copy of his rabies vaccination. You may also want to ask your veterinarian if the particular part of the country to which you are traveling requires additional vaccinations suitable for that area.

By Car

When traveling in a car, your dog should always travel in a safely secured crate. As with his crate at home, make sure that your dog can comfortably stand up and turn around in his car crate. If you travel extensively with your dog by car, you may want to invest in a metal crate for your home as well as an additional metal crate for your car.

When packing for your dog, bring a supply of his food, including extra food just in case you are unavoidably detained. Unexpected bad weather can also delay your return home. Feeding your dog while on the road is much easier if you make individual portions out the food and place each portion into its own sealed plastic bag. Then put all these bags into one bigger bag. Be sure to lock your dog's food so that he cannot get into it. If your dog needs medication, bring enough for your trip and a little extra just in case. Also be especially mindful never to leave your dog alone in a car due to the dangers of his overheating—which can happen much more quickly than you think even with the windows open. You may also want to bring an extra collar and leash as backups. Many people hook the spare collar and leash to the dog's car crate.

To prepare ahead for any emergency, including a car accident, write out your emergency information on an index card, put the index card into a bag, and affix the bag to the car crate out of the reach of your dog. The emergency information should include your name, address, and phone number; your veterinarian's information; a person to notify in case of an emergency if you are not available; your dog's name; the type of food he eats as well as the amount and time he eats; and any other important information about your dog, including any medications he needs, any special words he responds to, and which obedience commands he knows.

Remember to stop at least every two hours or whenever your dog lets you know he has to relieve himself. Be sure to pick up after your dog. Whenever you are going to take your dog out of the car, be vigilant about first securing him on his leash. Also, never leave your dog unattended in the car.

By Plane

Traveling by plane is a little more complicated than car travel. Every airline has different requirements that seem to change on an almost daily basis. Call ahead and find out your specific airline's regulations. In general, most adult dogs will need a medical certification from a veterinarian within about ten days of their flight. However, puppies less than eight or nine weeks old may not need this medical certificate.

You will need to arrive at the airport way in advance of the flight's departure time. Be sure to thoroughly exercise your dog before turning him over to the airline personnel. Dogs can fly alone or on the same flight as you. If you are flying an adult dog, you will need to bring him to the airport along with a hard plastic crate properly sized to him. He must be able to sit and turn around comfortably. You can give him a soft toy and a pad for his crate, or else put in shredded newspaper. There are also rules about how much food you need to put into a

Multi-Dog Tip

Although it is possible to compete with several dogs at the same event, most people find that they and their dogs do better if they only compete with one dog in one event each day. Some of these people decide to show one of their dogs on one day and a different dog the next day.

double-sealed plastic bag and tape to the top of his crate as well as how to handle his drinking requirements. And there are more rules about the identifying information you must provide and tape to the top of his crate.

Adult Aussies must fly in cargo. This means that if the weather is very hot, your dog cannot not fly. If the weather is very cold, your dog also cannot fly. These temperature extremes apply both to the flight's place of departure and to the place of arrival.

There are now a few more options for flying your dog. Certain airlines only transport dogs and they are kept where passengers are usually seated, and the dogs are accompanied by people who watch over them during the flight.

If you are flying with a puppy who is eight weeks old and who fits into a soft-sided bag under your airline seat, you can pay extra to take your puppy onboard the plane with you as a carry-on. Remember to take your puppy out of the bag while it goes through the baggage X-ray. You will need to take water and some of his food onboard with you just in case the food you packed for him in your checked luggage gets lost.

When you are flying a puppy or dog alone and are not also on the flight, stay at the airport until his flight actually departs. Then call the person who is picking up your puppy or dog to let her know the estimated time of arrival, especially if the flight is delayed. Ask her to call you once she actually picks up your puppy or dog. This gives peace of mind to all concerned parties, especially given the unpredictability of modern air travel.

Accommodations

You can find many hotels that allow your dog to stay in your room. Some of these hotels require a nonrefundable pet deposit at the time of checkin. Almost all of them ask that you never leave your dog alone in the room—which you should not do anyway. Be sure to bring a crate so that you can crate your dog while you are sleeping and cannot watch over him. You can also bring an old sheet to cover the hotel's bedspread.

Most major hotel chains have websites that tell you if dogs are allowed and the conditions under which they are allowed to stay. In addition, the American Automobile Association (AAA), which requires a fee to join, can provide a list of dog-friendly hotels.

If you can't travel with your dog, consider hiring a pet sitter.

Traveling Without Your Dog

If you are not able to take your Aussie with you, either by car or by plane, you must then arrange for his care in your absence. You have several options: You can hire a pet sitter to come into your house and stay there while you are gone, which can be an expensive option. Alternatively, you can board your dog which, although costly, is usually less expensive than hiring a pet sitter. Either way, your veterinarian, training instructor, or friends with dogs can point you toward a reliable pet sitter or boarding kennel. Be sure to give either the pet sitter or the boarding kennel your emergency contact information.

Pet Sitter

Before using a pet sitter, you may want to ask your family or friends if your dog can stay with them—either in your home or theirs. If this is not an option, then you can find a pet sitter by asking your veterinarian, your training instructor, friends with dogs, or your breeder. When you use a pet sitter, you need to interview her before you hire her. Ask her about her credentials, how long she has been pet sitting, whether she is insured, and if she is familiar with Australian Shepherds. In addition, ask her if she would be willing to walk your dog and, if so, how often. If she prefers to just let your dog out in your yard, find out how often she will do this each day. It is always safer to have a pet sitter let your dog out in your own yard than to permit her to walk your dog. Be clear to explain to the pet sitter how many times a day and for how long you want her to tend to your dog. If you want her to also stay overnight in your house, give her clear instructions about what you expect her to do (or not do) while there. Ask her about her fees and also for references.

Boarding Kennel

If you choose to board your dog, you can find a boarding kennel by asking your veterinarian, training instructor, breeder, and friends. Visit the boarding kennel before you leave your dog there. Make sure that the facility is clean, that the dogs look healthy and happy, and that they have clean bowls of fresh water. Find out about the total number of dogs that can be boarded there at one time. Ask how often the dogs are walked or if you have to pay extra for walks. Some boarding kennels offer playtime for an additional fee. Make sure that they have a veterinarian on call or available 24 hours a day, 7 days a week. Ask what vaccinations the kennel requires your dog to have, such as the kennel cough vaccination.

Doggy Day Care

Doggy day care can be a great option, especially for people who work full time away from the house. Using doggy day care can be especially good for puppies and young adults as a means of obtaining additional socialization for them while you are working. As with finding a pet sitter or a boarding kennel, you can find good doggy day care by asking your veterinarian, training instructor, friends, or breeder. Visit the day care center and make the same observations and ask the same questions that you would for a boarding kennel. Ask the people who are in charge essentially the same questions you would ask a pet sitter. Some doggy day care centers will, for an additional and often high fee, pick up and return your dog for you.

PART III

SENIOR YEARS

CHAPTER 12

FINDING YOUR AUSTRALIAN SHEPHERD SENIOR

There is just something special about a senior dog. They have a certain nobility and dignity in their eyes. At around the age of eight years, most Australian Shepherds noticeably begin to slow down. They are considered to be seniors when they reach the age of ten. Although the average lifespan of an Australian Shepherd is 10 to 12 years, they can live to be over 15 years old.

ADOPTING A SENIOR

There are many positives about adopting a senior dog, but as with any big decision, there can also be negatives. On balance, however, those who do adopt a senior dog find that the positives far outweigh the negatives.

The Positives

One of the main advantages of adopting a senior dog is that they do not have the high energy and activity level of a younger dog, especially a puppy. They tend to need shorter walks. They require your attention and time but not as much as a younger dog does. Many are perfectly happy with a short walk around the block and practicing a trick or two, and then they are content to nap by your feet as you do something else.

Puppies require an enormous amount of time in terms of socialization and initial training. When in the house, you constantly have to supervise them. Even adults need socialization time and training in basic and intermediate obedience commands as well as how to act in your house. But many seniors already know all this.

Most seniors will not bother to jump up on you or your visitors. They also won't spend the time or energy to dig up your yard or under your fence. They probably can no longer jump out of your yard anyway. Many know not to chew or be destructive in your house. A lot of seniors are already crate trained and housetrained. They may already know how to be in the house alone. All these things can make life with a senior most enjoyable. Instead of

Want to Know More?

For tips on training a senior Aussie, see Chapter 13: Care of Your Australian Shepherd Senior.

Senior dogs still enjoy training. Although they cannot jump as high as they once did, or even at all, there are still many activities you can do with them. Many especially like to learn new tricks that are not very physically strenuous.

teaching and training him in the fundamentals, you can simply relax together and enjoy each other's company.

Another huge advantage is that you do not have to constantly watch a senior to make sure that he is behaving in your house. You will not have to race around your house after a naughty dog who insists on stealing your socks as you try to get dressed in the morning. Seniors may not even have all their teeth, but they certainly will not make you suffer through their destructive teething phase as do puppies.

The majority of senior dogs are simply far easier to live with than a puppy or even an adult is. By this stage of their lives, most of them do not have the energy to get into the types of trouble that puppies and young adults constantly manage to create. A little of your time goes a long way with a senior dog.

You may find that your senior accepts being groomed and bathed without a fuss. He may love car rides and even visits to the veterinarian. His daily walks can be much shorter and certainly more enjoyable if he already knows how to walk nicely on a leash. Senior dogs generally do not lunge on a leash enough to make their owners fall down, which can occasionally happen with young adult dogs.

Because of the reduced energy level of seniors, many do not miss their former competitive loves. They do not particularly want to participate in many sports and activities. However, even senior Australian Shepherds need a job to do. Seniors are especially suited to becoming therapy dogs. They are much calmer than puppies and adults. They love going out and about to different hospitals and assisted living facilities. The people living there light up when they see a well-mannered therapy dog and love to fuss over him; in turn, a dog of any age loves being fussed over. There is truly something special watching frail, elderly people enjoy petting and talking to a senior dog. Maybe what makes their interaction so special is that both are seniors.

Many people feel that adopting a senior dog is the highest act of kindness. Adorable puppies are always the first to be adopted. People just love taking home a ball of fur, even if they are aware of the tremendous time commitment involved in properly raising a puppy. Some people are also perfectly happy to

Multi-Dog Tip

While many senior dogs get along well with puppies, sometimes puppies are simply too much for a senior dog—especially one who might not be steady on his feet or who has a touch of arthritis. In these cases, you should not let both your senior dog and your puppy out in the back yard together. An overly rambunctious puppy may accidentally knock over your senior.

The majority of senior dogs are simply far easier to live with than a puppy or even an adult is.

adopt an adult who is old enough to hopefully have had some training but not so old that he can no longer be very active. These people may be active themselves and enjoy the company of participating in various activities with their adult dog.

But finding a home for a senior dog is an entirely different proposition. The majority of people looking to adopt a dog do not want to take home a senior. The simple fact is that a senior dog does not have as many years left to live as does a puppy or an adult. For this reason alone, though, some people feel that

they *should* take home a senior dog—because no one else will. They do so as an act of kindness.

The Negatives

A senior dog is, by definition, an older dog. As such, he will not live with you for as long as a young puppy will. Further, he comes with a history that you may or may not know. Since some people are too lazy to bother to properly socialize their puppy or adult dog, the senior dog may not have been properly socialized when he was younger. It is possible but far more difficult for you to overcome these limitations at this point in his life. Such senior dogs may not be good around children, a person of a particular sex (especially if they were raised by a single owner), other dogs, or even cats.

Similarly, if a senior dog has rarely, if ever, been bathed or groomed, he may strongly object to being in a bathtub or even to a light touch of a brush. He may not like being combed, having his eyes and ears cleaned, or having his teeth brushed. He may put up a fight when you try to clip his nails. He may be extremely difficult when you try to put him into a car, and especially when you take him to visit the vet to be examined.

One of the most negative aspects about adopting a senior dog is that he may be in declining health. You may have to increase your visits to the veterinarian to monitor his health conditions. You may also have to give him certain medications for those conditions. All these things can become quite costly over time.

The senior dog may also not have any training. He may not be crate trained and may become overly anxious and even destructive when you first try to crate train him. If he has been a kennel dog all his life, he probably is not even housetrained. Furthermore, he may have some destructive behaviors around the house, such as chewing and jumping up on people. He may be a compulsive barker. He may be a confirmed fence digger, but chances are low that he will still be able to jump a fence. He may not know how to walk nicely on a leash without pulling. He may also be

If you adopt a senior from a breeder, you'll know about his background.

aggressive toward people or other dogs and even try to nip them out of fear.

An untrained senior dog will not know the basic obedience commands of *come*, *down*, or *sit*. He most likely will not ever have been introduced to the intermediate obedience commands of *heel*, *stay*, *down-stay*, *sit-stay*, or *stand*. As such, he will be more difficult for you to manage.

Even if trained, a senior dog is physically not able to participate in a lot of sports and activities, especially competitive ones. Agility and obedience require that a dog be able to jump. This can, even at lower heights, be troublesome for senior dogs. They are probably not able to move well enough to show in conformation either. Even canine freestyle requires a certain body flexibility that many seniors are no longer capable of doing. Senior dogs are, for the most part, not the right age for most competitive sports and activities.

HOW TO FIND A SENIOR AUSSIE

There are many options open to you in terms of how to find a senior dog. In fact, it is probably far easier to find a senior dog than it is to find an adult, and it's certainly much easier than finding a puppy. The demand for senior dogs is just not that high.

Many breeders will try to find good homes for their senior dogs, especially after their breeding lives are over. Often breeders say that

they want their senior dog to finish out his life sleeping on a sofa as a beloved household pet. This is an excellent way to find a senior dog, because you will know the dog's complete history. In most cases, you will also know the history of the dog's parents. Knowledge of a dog's personal and family health issues may help you to recognize the health problems he may develop and hopefully solve them before they become too severe.

Another place to find a senior dog is through a rescue organization or an animal shelter. People who work at these places are especially thankful when someone deliberately chooses to take home one of their senior dogs. They know that their senior dogs are the least likely candidates for adoptions.

CHAPTER 13

CARE OF YOUR AUSTRALIAN SHEPHERD SENIOR

Just as puppies and adults have certain requirements for their care, seniors also need special help from you. Australian Shepherds begin to slow down around the age of eight or so, although of course there are individual variations. By the age of ten, most Australian Shepherds are considered seniors. The average life span of an Australian Shepherd is 10 to 12 years, although many can live longer. It is up to you to recognize the signs of aging so you can give your senior Aussie the appropriate care.

SIGNS OF AGING

One day, you will wake up and look at your senior Australian Shepherd and wonder when he became an old dog. Old age is not a disease; it is a normal life process that occurs very gradually over time. If you live with a puppy and also a senior, then these signs of aging will be more apparent to you.

The most obvious sign of aging in a dog is that his coat becomes flecked with white, normally around the eyes and on the muzzle. As the dog continues to age, these white hairs appear on the chest and rear, and eventually the flecks of white hair turn into patches of white hair. Often, those not familiar with Aussies think that gray merle dogs are old because their coats have gray in them. Some lines of gray merle dogs will grow darker and more gray every year, starting from the first time they blow their coat.

A more subtle sign of aging in a dog is the loss of body fat and muscle tone. This can be especially noticeable on a dog's hips, which are lightly padded with body fat and muscle in adults but appear bony in seniors. Senior dogs do not get up or lie down as quickly as they once did. They may no longer shadow your movements around the house.

Old dogs do not move as fast or as much, nor do they jump as high as they did as youngsters. An old dog may stand at the top of the basement staircase watching you descend, rather than go down the stairs with you. He may be hesitant about going up stairs as well. Senior dogs do not see as well and may lose some of their depth perception. You can apply a thick strip of white duct tape on the edge of the stairs to help him see better.

A lot of elderly dogs begin to lose their hearing as well. If you open the refrigerator door and he comes over, then he can still hear.

Senior dogs simply do not have as high a metabolism as they once did.

But if this same dog no longer comes when you call him, he may have developed selective hearing loss but not deafness.

Some older dogs may eat more slowly or even not finish their food. Your dog may be bothered by irritations on his gum or may have developed a bad tooth.

Senior dogs always sleep more than when they were young. If they have some hearing loss, they may not wake up as quickly when there is a noise. Even when they are awake, they are far less active.

FEEDING

You will need to make some feeding adjustments for your senior dog. These changes may include what to feed him and his feeding schedule.

What to Feed

Senior dogs simply do not have as high a metabolism as they once did and therefore do not need or generally even want to eat as much as they did when in their prime. It is normal to notice changes in a senior's appetite. A dog who once wolfed down his food may develop into a picky eater. If this happens, it is a good idea to first check your dog's gums and mouth to make sure that nothing is amiss. Old teeth are more prone to cracking, so you may want your veterinarian to also take a look. Any normal decrease in appetite should be gradual. If your senior suddenly stops eating, it is usually a sign of a health issue that requires a visit to the veterinarian.

Once you determine that your dog's teeth and gums are healthy, you may have to make his food more appetizing while bearing in mind that his overall caloric intake should not be drastically increased. If you feed kibble, you may want to add some warm—not hot—water. You can also add a spoonful or two of canned food to make the kibble smell and taste more appealing. Many dogs go crazy over canned green tripe, which contains excellent probiotics for digestion and is extremely healthy in general.

As your senior continues to age, his appetite may further decrease. Another way to make his food more tempting is by pouring some chicken or beef broth over his kibble, instead of water. You can also cut up tiny pieces of cooked chicken to add to the meal. At this stage, some owners start home cooking for their dog. Often the smell of the food being prepared makes a senior dog more interested in eating. As we discussed in Chapter 7, there are many cookbooks available on how to home-cook for your dog, and some of them have special recipes just for senior dogs. If you have other dogs in your household, take care that they do not steal your senior's special meal out of his bowl.

Even though most senior dogs tend to have less body fat, they can easily become obese, because their metabolism and activity level are lower. Some people prefer to decrease the amount of food they feed their senior dog but continue to feed him what he has always eaten. Other people elect to purchase food with lower protein and fat levels specially formulated for senior dogs. In either case, you may want to give your senior dog a multiple vitamin, as he is not able to absorb nutrients as well from his food.

Feeding Schedule

As a general rule, Australian Shepherds know their feeding schedule to the second. As long as your senior is still eating the same number of times a day and at the same times each day, there is no need to make any adjustments to his feeding schedule. If your Australian Shepherd stops eating much at all, then he surely needs to go to the veterinarian.

A senior dog will probably eat more slowly than he did as a puppy—everything tends to slow down with an older dog. As long as he keeps up a steady pace and cleans his bowl, his feeding schedule is probably appropriate for his needs.

GROOMING

A dog's skin becomes more sensitive as he ages. A dog who used to enjoy being combed and brushed may now pull away from you. He may even run and try to hide when he sees you pull out the comb and brush. Still, he needs his weekly grooming sessions.

It may be easier on both of you if you split his weekly grooming sessions into a few smaller sessions over the course of the week, rather than attempting to groom him all at once. While you are brushing and combing, be extra careful not to pull his hair.

By the Numbers

Australian Shepherds reach middle age by the time they are eight. By ten years old, they are considered elderly. On average, Aussies live between 10 and 12 years.

Another issue that can affect grooming is that some seniors cannot stand up for long periods of time. You can try to groom him on the grooming table, but at this stage of his life, you will have to pick him up to get him on and off the table. He is too old now to jump that high. You might place an old beach towel on your sofa and try grooming him there. Another option is to groom him on the floor, but this will be harder on you.

In any event, do not ask your senior to stand for long periods of time. It may be too uncomfortable for him now. Most dogs are

Want to Know More?

How to find a professional groomer is discussed in Chapter 6: Australian Shepherd Grooming Needs.

able to sit longer than they can stand. If you have trained your dog to lie on his belly and sides, he should be more comfortable during grooming. You can generally use a piece of food to help him into these different positions.

Because senior Aussies tend to lie around and sleep a lot, they may develop mats in their coats. If possible, gently break apart the mats using your fingers. For tougher mats, you may have to use scissors to cut them out of your dog's coat, but be careful not to accidentally cut his skin. If you prefer not to do

Health care is especially important during the senior years.

Keep your senior physically and mentally stimulated.

this yourself, take your dog to a professional groomer.

When grooming your senior dog, you now have one extra and important chore to perform. Older dogs can develop lumps and bumps all over their body, many of which are not medically significant. However, be sure to keep track of these lumps and bumps and notice if any appear to be growing. Report those to your veterinarian, but don't wait for your senior's checkup if they are growing quickly.

Bathing a senior dog can be difficult. You will have to help your dog into and out of the bathtub. He probably does not need to be bathed as much as he did when he was young, because he is no longer as active—or as naughty! (Senior dogs generally do not dig in gardens.) However, as he ages, he may begin to have problems keeping himself as clean when eliminating, especially when urinating. Instead of giving him a complete bath, you can purchase a dry shampoo that does not require water and can be wiped off without rinsing. After you wipe off the dry shampoo, use a little water on the area to prevent any stickiness.

HEALTH CARE

Health care is especially important during the senior years. In fact, good preventative care calls for seniors to be taken to the veterinarian for a checkup every six months. Also, your dog may develop certain illnesses common to senior dogs.

Arthritis cannot be cured; it can only be managed.

Preventive Care: Senior Checkups

One of the most important aspects of preventive care for seniors is to increase checkups to every six months instead of taking your dog annually. These checkups are similar to those that he had as an adult, but since a senior's health condition can change quickly, he needs to be seen by the veterinarian more frequently.

Your veterinarian will usually weigh your dog first, because a weight increase or decrease may indicate a health issue. She will take your dog's temperature. She will look at his eyes, in his ears, and in his mouth, noting the condition of his teeth and gums. She will check his body all over and feel for lumps or bumps. She will also feel your dog's leg and shoulder joints to see if there are any areas of excessive heat, indicative of possible arthritis. She may ask you to walk your dog around, so that she can see any changes in his gait, which also could point to arthritis.

Your vet will ask you about any changes in your dog's eating and elimination habits, including amount and frequency, and she'll want to do a fecal test. She will then ask you about any behavioral changes in your dog, including his overall activity level and sleeping habits.

Then it's your turn to ask questions. You may want to discuss whether or not your veterinarian feels that your dog is at the proper weight. If he is not, she may suggest changes in what you are feeding him, the amount you are feeding him, and the number of times he is fed. If you have found any lumps and bumps on your dog's body, now is the time to show them to her. You can discuss the medications your dog is taking and ask if the dosages are still correct. You can also ask your veterinarian if she has any special advice that will help you to take the best possible care of your senior dog.

In addition, at each of these checkups, have your veterinarian do a full blood panel test and urine test. This is one of the best ways to monitor a senior's overall health. Signs of ill health or disease can sometimes be detected in a dog's blood or urine before you notice them. It would also be a good idea to do a thyroid test, as older dogs may develop hypothyroidism.

Physical Health

Your senior's health care includes ensuring that he remains stimulated physically. As such, you still need to walk your dog every day; however, you will probably need to shorten the length of his walks. Be especially careful about walking your senior when it is very hot or very cold, as he is more likely to feel temperature extremes. You should also make sure that he has proper footing on his walks. If the sidewalks are covered with ice or snow, it is not a good time to walk your senior dog. He does not have the muscle tone to manage these conditions and, without good footing, could easily fall and get hurt.

Mental Health

As for his mental stimulation, seniors enjoy daily training sessions as much as puppies do (or maybe even more). After all, they've had these daily training sessions their entire lives. While you cannot ask your Aussie to do what he once did, you can certainly focus on teaching him easy tricks that are fun for both of you. When visitors come, you and your senior dog can perform these tricks—your visitors will then make a great fuss over his absolute

brilliance. We'll discuss training your senior dog later in this chapter.

Senior Illnesses

The aging process wears a senior's body out. Senior dogs are more likely to develop certain illnesses, including arthritis, canine cognitive disorder (CCD), cataracts, congestive heart failure, and Cushing's disease.

Arthritis

If your dog lives long enough, regardless of the breed, he may well develop arthritis in his old age. Arthritis (also called osteoarthritis) can have different causes. Overly stressed joints are more likely to develop arthritis, for example poorly formed or dysplastic hips, joints near severely strained or torn ligaments or tendons, and joints near bones that were broken. Many believe that dogs who contract Lyme disease are more likely to develop early arthritis. Sometimes the joints in elderly dogs simply wear out. There may even be a genetic component to arthritis.

An arthritic dog may have trouble getting up or lying down. He may be reluctant to change positions. He may limp or walk with a stiff-legged gait or even hop slightly on one leg or another. He may not want to walk up or down stairs or even accompany you into the car. Overall, he just is not moving right.

In hopes of preventing or arresting the development of arthritis , many owners give their senior dogs supplements containing a combination of glucosamine and chondroitin, which are purported to promote cartilage growth. Oils high in omega fatty acids, such as salmon oil, may also help.

Arthritis cannot be cured; it can only be managed. Arthritis can result in painful inflammation. Depending on your dog's level of pain, your veterinarian may recommend one of several medications. Some dogs respond well to buffered aspirin, while others need shots of prednisone into the affected joint. Buffered aspirin can damage a dog's delicate digestive system and should be used with caution and only under a veterinarian's care.

If your dog appears to be in pain despite any of these treatments, your veterinarian may need to prescribe actual pain medication to control the pain. Be aware that some pain medications will upset your dog's stomach to the point that he will refuse to eat. Liquid pain medications may be easier for older dogs to tolerate.

Alternative therapies, which we discussed in Chapter 8: Australian Shepherd Health and Wellness, can be especially useful as supplemental treatments for arthritis. Many older dogs with arthritis respond well to

acupuncture treatments and chiropractic adjustments. Physical therapy such as swimming may also help, as swimming has a low impact on joints. In addition, it is important that arthritic seniors still go on daily walks and move around; you will just need to shorten the walks.

Canine Cognitive Disorder (CCD)

CCD is an age-related disorder that causes the deterioration of cognitive abilities. It is often compared to Alzheimer's disease in humans. Usually CCD appears gradually and becomes worse over time. Dogs with CCD can show a variety of symptoms, including acting a bit "senile." Some may forget that they are housetrained; others may shuffle around the house with a confused expression or even get

Older dogs enjoy comfy places to sleep.

stuck in a corner, unable to find their way out. Certain dogs with CCD get their sleep patterns mixed up and start sleeping more during the day and not very much at night. Some dogs with CCD start behaving inappropriately. For example, some may start guarding their food, bones, or toys. And they may act like they no longer know people that they should know well.

All is not right in the world of a dog with CCD. His confusion and inability to understand why he is so confused may lead him to become aggressive. He could also start engaging in obsessive-compulsive behaviors, such as excessive barking at absolutely nothing or even licking himself until his skin bleeds.

Your veterinarian can tell you if your dog has CCD by ruling out all other possibilities; there is no test that can positively affirm that a dog has CCD. If the diagnosis is CCD, your vet can provide you with medication that may help slow the progression. In addition, she may suggest giving your dog more fatty acids and vitamin C. Dogs with CCD require extreme patience. Be sure to remain patient with him even if he becomes increasingly difficult.

Cataracts

Australian Shepherds can develop juvenile cataracts, which develop at a young age. However, senior Australian Shepherds, as well as older dogs in general, can develop old-age cataracts. The symptoms and treatment for old age cataracts are the same as those for juvenile cataracts (see Chapter 8 for more information). The only exception is that an older dog will be able to undergo the anesthesia necessary for cataract removal only if he is in sufficiently good health.

Old age cataracts should not be confused with nuclear sclerosis. In both cataracts and nuclear sclerosis, the lens of the eye looks cloudy. Unlike cataracts, nuclear sclerosis does not generally at first impair a dog's ability to see—except, perhaps, for depth perception; in effect, your dog needs reading glasses.

Your veterinarian, or a veterinary ophthalmologist, can examine and test your dog's eyes to determine if your dog has old age cataracts or nuclear sclerosis. The condition of nuclear sclerosis cannot be cured or even managed, but it is also likely that your dog's vision will not be negatively affected except for extreme cases.

Congestive Heart Failure

Another problem in senior dogs is congestive heart failure, where the heart can no longer efficiently circulate the blood correctly, so blood begins to build up around the heart. It is sometimes caused by a leak in one of the heart values. Congestive heart failure is a progressive disease. For example, it may begin as a minor heart murmur. In advanced stages, the dog will have labored breathing and may even cough, especially after running. In the final stage, the dog has no energy and may even faint if he attempts to run.

Congestive heart failure is another disease that cannot be cured, only managed. Your veterinarian may give your dog medications to strengthen his heart muscles and to help lessen the amount of fluid building up around his heart. As with most heart conditions, you should put your Aussie on a low-sodium diet. Also, your dog still needs daily walks, but you will need to shorten them and make sure that he does not become overexerted. You definitely want to make sure that your dog is not stressed. It is especially important to keep your dog's teeth and gums healthy, since infections in the mouth can travel easily to the heart.

Cushing's Disease

Another disease of senior dogs is Cushing's

disease, or hyperadrenocorticism. In Cushing's disease, the dog's pituitary gland becomes overactive and begins to make too much pituitary hormone (ACTH), which causes the adrenal gland to produce an overabundance of glucocorticoids. There is also a less prevalent type of Cushing's disease in which the adrenal gland becomes overactive and also results in too many glucocorticoids.

With either type of Cushing's disease, the symptoms appear gradually and increase in severity over time. A dog with Cushing's disease will start drinking a tremendous amount of water and therefore need to urinate often. He may even urinate accidentally in the house. He may try to eat more and will gain weight, especially in his stomach area. He may start to lose hair, and his skin may seem thinner. The problem with many of these symptoms is that they can also be typical of an aging dog who does not suffer from Cushing's disease.

Your veterinarian can diagnosis Cushing's disease based on certain tests, including a full blood panel and urine analysis. For Cushing's disease caused by an overactive adrenal gland, she may need to rule out a tumor on that gland.

Training Tidbit

A senior dog cannot react as quickly as a puppy. When you ask him to do something, expect that he'll be a little slower in responding. He probably does not see or hear as well either, so you may have to move closer to him or raise your voice a little to help him.

If diagnosed, Cushing's disease cannot be cured, but it can be managed through medication. These dogs will remain on this medication for the remainder of their lives and will need to be tested periodically to make sure that the levels of medication are appropriate. However, if the dog has a tumor on his adrenal gland, the tumor may have to be surgically removed.

TRAINING

Although your senior Australian Shepherd may not be as physically active as he was as a young pup, he still is mentally active and needs daily mental stimulation. Moreover, he certainly needs attention from you. Training him a little every day is a great way for you to achieve both goals.

The key to training a senior dog is to make training easier for him. Remember that he can no longer do those unbelievable flying leaps and jumps. He may need to take his time to sit or lie down or to stand up from either of those positions. He may not be able to hold any one position for very long. It is up to you to figure out his physical limitations and then train him within those limitations.

For example, you may ask him to do a *sit-stay* for only five seconds. You may request that he perform a *down-stay* for 30 seconds. You can heel him in big circles instead of sharp right or left turns. You can also walk more slowly with him while heeling. When you call him to you, you can also clap your hands in case his eyesight or hearing is slightly impaired. He does not have to do these things in the same way he once did—in fact, he cannot. But he can still do most of the things you taught him. It's just that now he must take his time about doing them and should not be expected to be as perfect.

Another tip is to do activities together that may not necessarily be "traditional" training

Multi-Dog Tip

Senior dogs can be training role models for younger dogs for basic obedience commands. After putting your younger dog in a crate in the training area, ask your senior dog to do a basic obedience command, and then make a huge fuss over him. Your younger dog will be very eager to learn the same basic command.

but still stimulate his mind. If you have already certified your Aussie to be a therapy dog, now may be the ideal time to do more therapy work together. Those who do therapy work find it immensely rewarding and fulfilling; it is a way for them to give something back to their community. How to get involved in therapy work was discussed in Chapter 11: Australian Shepherd Sports and Activities.

Almost all dogs, and especially senior dogs, love to go on car rides. You can try to find appropriate new places to go. You can put your senior dog in your car and then go off to a park. You can then walk around and let him see and hear all that is going on there. Maybe your senior would enjoy watching a ball game at a local school yard with you. If he has been well socialized, he will probably enjoy simply being with you around the activity of people in new places.

You can take your senior dog to visit friends and family who will appreciate him. He truly will have fun when all those people pet him and tell him what a wonderful dog he has become. They will probably try to stuff him with treats, so you may want to bring your own and give people individual portions to give to your dog. This way, he will not overeat,

which is important if he has a tendency to gain weight.

You can still throw a tennis ball in the yard for your senior dog. Australian Shepherds generally enjoy a good game of tennis ball throwing. However, now you need to keep these sessions brief. Also, you must adjust your throws so that they are shorter and lower to the ground or so they just roll. You do not want your senior to attempt one of his famous flying leaps, which might now injure him. In a multi-dog household, you probably should have only your senior dog out in the yard with you when playing ball. The younger dogs are much faster and will get to the ball before he does. Alone with you, your senior can be successful.

Figure out your senior's physical limitations, and then train him within those limitations.

CHAPTER 14

END-OF-LIFE ISSUES

Loving and caring for a dog entails many responsibilities, the last and most difficult of which involve end-of-life issues.

WHEN IS IT TIME?

There is no right or wrong time for euthanizing your beloved dog; this is an intensely personal and individual decision. Sometimes the decision is no longer yours, as when a dog is severely injured in a car accident and is put on life support. Some senior dogs, like elderly people, simply die gently in their sleep during the night. Some dogs deteriorate slowly over time, and you have trouble even noticing that they are failing until one day you look at them and realize that they are not doing well. Other dogs suffer a sudden, horrific event such as a stroke. In other words, in some cases you have time to prepare yourself to make this life or death decision, and in other cases, you have absolutely no time whatsoever to even think about it.

Most of the time, however, you will be faced with the ultimate decision of deciding if it is time to put your dog to sleep. People who have been through this sad experience often say that the dog tells them when it is time by a certain expression in his eyes. The eyes tell them that the body is just worn out and he has had enough.

Most people use a sort of quality-of-life evaluation to make this decision. They want their dog to be able to enjoy the simple joys in a healthy dog's life, such as being able to eat, eliminate, and walk enough to be considered mobile. Once a dog can no longer do these basic life activities, they believe their dog is not enjoying life and that the time has unfortunately come. Their philosophy can be summed up as follows: No dog should ever be permitted by his owner to starve to death. No dog should ever be allowed by his owner to lie in his own waste. No dog should ever spend his final days immobile because he is unable to get up and walk even a few steps.

An option many people rely on is a consultation with their veterinarian. If you have any doubts about whether or not the time for euthanasia has arrived, take your dog to the veterinarian. Have your veterinarian do a thorough examination of him. Then you can ask her opinion about whether or not she believes your dog is in pain and should be put out of it. The proper form of this question, for ethical reasons, is not the following: "Should I

Hospice care can make a senior's last days as comfortable as possible.

euthanize my dog now?" Instead, the following more indirect question will elicit your veterinarian's opinion: "If he was your dog, would you euthanize him now?" Since you already have a solid, long-term relationship with your veterinarian, and she has helped you to care for your dog for his entire life, you can rely on your veterinarian to be honest with you. Veterinarians want to do only what is best for your dog.

In the final analysis, euthanasia may be about doing what is best for your dog. It is not necessarily about what is doing best for you.

HOSPICE AND EUTHANASIA

If your senior dog is failing but is not yet suffering, you may decide to provide hospice

for him in your own home. Essentially, you, after consultation with your veterinarian, may decide that there is nothing more medically that can be done for your dog. You will then try to make your dog's final days or perhaps even weeks as comfortable as possible.

Hospice care means never allowing a dog to suffer. Hospice is all about allowing you the time to say good-bye to your dog and him to you. However, if your dog begins to suffer, then hospice care is no longer a viable option; it is replaced with euthanasia.

When a dog is euthanized, you can be present in the room or not as you prefer. If you are in the room, you can speak to and even hold your dog as he is being put to sleep. In most cases, you will be asked to sign a document authorizing that the veterinarian euthanize your dog. The veterinarian will again ask you if you are sure that now is the time. A veterinarian will euthanize a dog only if she also agrees with you.

The euthanasia procedure itself is fast and painless for the dog. It consists of two shots. The first shot is a tranquilizer to relax your dog. The second shot causes your dog's heart to stop. Some dogs give a long sigh, but this sign is only air expressing out of their lungs; they have already passed. In some cases, a dog who is newly deceased may eliminate, so many vets put paper towels between the dog's legs. You will be able to remain in the room to say your final good-bye.

You then have a few options about what to do with your dog's body. If your jurisdiction permits, you can bury the dog in your

Training Tidbit

As a dog's time nears, reward him with special praise and a favorite treat simply for looking up at you. He is doing the best he can and, most of all, he is expressing his love for you with his eyes.

back yard. If not, then some areas have pet cemeteries exclusively for pet burials. A common alternative is to have your dog cremated. Your dog's ashes will be delivered in a wooden box with a plate containing his name. Some people also request snips of their

Other dogs in your home may grieve after the loss of a dog.

Multi-Dog Tip

If you have multiple dogs, including a senior dog nearing the end of his life together with a puppy in your household, be alert to protecting both of them. Some senior dogs at this stage may be in pain and may snap at or even hurt a puppy who approaches them. By the same token, a puppy trying to play may accidentally hurt a fragile senior.

dog's hair or even a mold of his paw print. You can keep the box containing your dog's ashes in your house, or you can bury his ashes in your yard. You can then achieve closure by placing a tombstone over your dog's grave complete with a personalized inscription.

GRIEF

Grief is a normal process following the loss of a beloved dog. Grief is also a highly individual process. Some people turn inward and grieve privately. Others find that being extremely busy helps them. Whatever you do to grieve, it will take some time to get over the loss of your pet. There is no right or wrong way to grieve, and

For some, the best way to overcome their grief is getting a new puppy.

Treasured Moments

No matter how many times you may lose a senior dog, it is never any easier. But each dog gives you treasured moments that you will remember and keep in your heart forever. His heart becomes part of yours.

no standard time for grieving.

If you have children, especially young children, they will also be grieving. They may not be old enough to fully understand the concept of death. The one thing you should never say to young children is that their dog ran away; this sad excuse of an explanation could create a feeling of rejection in children. You can, however, allow them to participate in a ceremony, especially if you buried your dog or his ashes. Perhaps you can even have a funeral. Everyone, including small children, can say a few words and even drop a rose or two onto your dog's grave.

Animals, especially other dogs in your household, may also be grieving. Your deceased dog was part of your household pack. The remaining dogs will have one of three reactions; namely, they will either be sad about the absence of your senior dog, they will appear to be happy about his loss, or they will show no change whatsoever in their behavior. Remember that grief is an individual process for dogs too. It may help some dogs to see the body of the deceased dog, while other dogs will not care. For grieving dogs, give them extra time and attention.

One thing that is sure to happen, however, is that if you have multiple dogs and one dies, then your pack structure will change. If your senior dog was the head of the pack, then the other dogs may jostle among themselves to establish the next pack leader. In addition, your dogs will notice that you are upset and may react by misbehaving. You need to remain in control of your dogs and make them feel that you are in charge no matter who among them may want to be in charge.

For everyone concerned, including family members, you, and any other household dogs, the best way to overcome grief may well be to get another Australian Shepherd. It is very hard to be sad when you are laughing at the antics of an Aussie puppy. And you will hardly have the time to be sad, since all your time and attention will be centered around raising your puppy.

50 FUN FACTS EVERY AUSTRALIAN SHEPHERD OWNER SHOULD KNOW

1. Australian Shepherds are an American, not an Australian, breed.

2. Many Australian Shepherds smile.

3. Some Australian Shepherds even grin.

4. This is a very active and athletic breed.

5. Australian Shepherds have a medium-length coat.

6. Australian Shepherds are a double-coated breed with both a topcoat and an undercoat.

7. Australian Shepherds shed.

8. Australian Shepherds are highly intelligent.

9. Australian Shepherds require daily physical and mental exercise.

10. Australian Shepherds have a great sense of humor and love to play.

11. Jay Sisler used his Australian Shepherds in a rodeo act.

12. Australian Shepherds appeared in a movie released by Walt Disney Productions called *Cow Dog*.

13. Australian Shepherds also starred in a movie released by Walt Disney Productions called *Stub: Best Cow Dog in the West*.

14. The Australian Shepherd Club of America (ASCA) offers registration privileges to Australian Shepherds.

15. The ASCA publishes a magazine every other month about the breed called *The Aussie Times*.

16. The American Kennel Club (AKC) also grants registration privileges to Australian Shepherds.

17. The United States Australian Shepherd Association (USASA) is the national affiliate club for the AKC.

18. The USASA publishes a magazine every two months about the breed called *The Australian Shepherd Journal*.

19. The average Australian Shepherd litter has about seven puppies.

20. Australian Shepherds are extremely versatile.

21. Australian Shepherds are highly trainable.

22. As a herding dog, Australian Shepherds need a job.

23. Australian Shepherds excel in performance events, including obedience, rally, agility, and flyball.

24. Some Australian Shepherds cannot tolerate the drug ivermectin, which is found in some common heartworm medications.

25. Some Australian Shepherds may develop eye problems.

26. Some Australian Shepherds may be afflicted with epilepsy.

27. Most male Australian Shepherds are about 20 to 23 inches at the withers.

28. Most female Australian Shepherds are about 18 to 21 inches at the withers.

29. It is very important to socialize Australian Shepherds.

30. Puppy kindergarten is a great class for starting socalization.

31. Some Australian Shepherds are born with natural bobtails; others are docked.

32. Most Australian Shepherds are bred naturally.

33. Most Australian Shepherds also whelp naturally.

34. Australian Shepherds live about 10 to 12 years.

35. Australian Shepherds can be one of four different colors.

36. Australian Shepherds can have a merle-colored coat.

37. Australian Shepherds can be blue or red merles. They can also be black or red tris.

38. The eyes of an Australian Shepherd can be brown or blue.

39. An Australian Shepherd can have one blue eye and one brown eye.

40. Within a single eye, Australian Shepherds can have flecks of another color.

41. The eye of an Australian Shepherd should be shaped like an almond.

42. As a herding dog, good feet are very important for an Australian Shepherd.

43. Most Australian Shepherds have a healthy appetite and are good eaters.

44. The front angles and the rear angles of an Australian Shepherd should be in balance.

45. The overall appearance of an Australian Shepherd should be moderate in nature.

46. Many Australian Shepherds love to play ball.

47. As a rule, Australian Shepherds are easy to housetrain.

48. Australian Shepherds are good, natural jumpers.

49. Australian Shepherds can be trained to herd stock such as cattle, sheep, and ducks.

50. Australian Shepherds require a lot of time and attention from their owners.

ASSOCIATIONS AND ORGANIZATIONS

Breed Clubs

American Kennel Club (AKC)
5580 Centerview Drive
Raleigh, NC 27606
Telephone: (919) 233-9767
Fax: (919) 233-3627
E-mail: info@akc.org
www.akc.org

Australian Shepherd Club of America (ASCA)
6091 E. State Hwy 21
Bryan, TX
Telephone: (979) 778-1082
E-mail: manager@asca.org
www.asca.org

Canadian Kennel Club (CKC)
200 Ronson Drive, Suite 400
Etobicoke, Ontario
M9W 6R4
Canada
Telephone: (416) 675-5511
Fax: (416) 675-6506
E-mail: information@ckc.ca
www.ckc.ca

Fédération Cynologique Internationale (FCI)
13 Place Albert 1er
B-6530 Thuin
Belgium
Telephone: 32 71 59 12 38
Fax: 32 71 59 22 29
E-mail: info@fci.be
www.fci.be

The Kennel Club
1-5 Clarges Street
Picadilly, London
W1J 8AB
United Kingdom
Telephone: 0844 463 3980
Fax: 020 7518 1058
www.thekennelclub.org.uk

United Kennel Club (UKC)
100 E. Kilgore Road
Kalamazoo, MI 49002-5584
Telephone: (269) 343-9020
Fax: (269) 343-7037
www.ukcdogs.com

The United States Australian Shepherd Association (USASA)
E-mail: slfonta@msn.com
www.australianshepherds.org

Grooming

The International Society of Canine Cosmetologists (ISCC)
2702 Covington Drive
Garland, TX 75040
Fax: (972) 530-3313
E-mail: iscc@petstylist.com
www.petstylist.com

National Dog Groomers Association of America, Inc. (NDGAA)
P.O. Box 101
Clark, PA 16113
Telephone: (724) 962-2711
Fax: (724) 962-1919
E-mail: ndgaa@
nationaldoggroomers.com
www.nationaldoggroomers.com

Pet Sitters

National Association of Professional Pet Sitters (NAPPS)
15000 Commerce Parkway, Suite C
Mt. Laurel, NJ 08054
Telephone: (856) 439-0324
E-mail: NAPPS@ahint.com
www.petsitters.org

Pet Sitters International
201 East King Street
King, NC 27021
Telephone: (336) 983-9222
Fax: (336) 983-5266
E-mail: info@petsit.com
www.petsit.com

Rescue Organizations and Animal Welfare Groups

American Humane Association (AHA)
63 Inverness Drive East
Englewood, CO 80112
Telephone: (800) 227-4645
Fax: (303) 792-5333
www.americanhumane.org

American Society for the Prevention of Cruelty to Animals (ASPCA)
424 E. 92nd Street
New York, NY 10128-6804
Telephone: (212) 876-7700
www.aspca.org

Canadian Federation of Humane Societies (CFHS)
102-30 Concourse Gate
Ottawa, ON K2E 7V7
Canada
Telephone: (888) 678-CFHS
Fax: (613)723-0252
E-mail: info@cfhs.ca
www.cfhs.ca

The Humane Society of the United States (HSUS)
2100 L Street, NW
Washington, DC 20037
Telephone: (202) 452-1100
www.humanesociety.org

Partnership for Animal Welfare
P.O. Box 1074
Greenbelt, MD 20768
Telephone: (301) 572-4729
E-mail: dogs@paw-rescue.org
www.paw-rescue.org

Royal Society for the Prevention of Cruelty to Animals (RSPCA)
Wilberforce Way
Southwater, Horsham,
West Sussex RH13 9R
United Kingdom
Telephone: 0300 123 4555
Fax: 0303 123 0100
vetfone: 0906 500 5500
www.rspca.org.uk

Sports

Agility Association of Canada (AAC)
RR#2
Lucan, Ontario N0N 2J0
Canada
Telephone: (519) 657-7636
www.aac.ca

North American Dog Agility Council (NADAC)
P.O. Box 1206
Colbert, OK 74733
E-mail: info@nadac.com
www.nadac.com

North American Flyball Association (NAFA)
1400 West Devon Avenue, #512
Chicago, IL 60660
Telephone/Fax: (800) 318-6312
E-mail: flyball@flyball.org
www.flyball.org

United States Dog Agility Association (USDAA)
P.O. Box 850955
Richardson, TX 75085-0955
Telephone: (972) 487-2200
Fax: (972) 231-9700
E-mail: info@usdaa.com
www.usdaa.com

The World Canine Freestyle Organization, Inc.
P.O. Box 350122
Brooklyn, NY 11235
Telephone: (718) 332-8336
Fax: (718) 646-2686
E-mail: WCFODOGS@aol.com
www.worldcaninefreestyle.org

Therapy

Delta Society Pet Partners Program
875 124th Ave. NE, Suite 101
Bellevue, WA 98005
Telephone: (425) 679-5500
Fax: (425) 679-5539
E-mail: info@deltasociety.org
www.deltasociety.org

Therapy Dogs Incorporated
P.O. Box 20227
Cheyenne, WY 82003
Telephone: (877) 843-7364
E-mail: therapydogsinc@
qwestoffice.net
www.therapydogs.com

Therapy Dogs International
88 Bartley Square
Flanders, NJ 07836
Telephone: (973) 252-9800
Fax: (973) 252-7171
E-mail: tdi@gti.net
www.tdi-dog.org

Training

American College of Veterinary Behaviorists (ACVB)
Dr. Bonnie V. Beaver, ACVB
Executive Director
Texas A&M University
College Station, TX 77843-4474
E-mail: info@dacvb.org
www.veterinarybehaviorists.org

Animal Behavior Society (ABS)
Indiana University
402 N. Park Ave.
Bloomington, IN 47408-2603
Telephone: (812) 856-5541
Fax: (812) 856-5542
E-mail: aboffice@indiana.edu
www.animalbehaviorsociety.org

Association of Pet Dog Trainers (APDT)
101 North Main St., Suite 610
Greenville, SC 29601
Telephone: (800) PET-DOGS
Fax: (864) 331-0767
E-mail: information@apdt.com
www.apdt.com

Certification Council for Pet Dog Trainers (CCPDT)
1350 Broadway, 17th Floor
New York, NY 10018
Telephone: (212) 356-0682
E-mail: administrator@ccpdt.org
www.ccpdt.org

International Association of Animal Behavior Consultants (IAABC)
565 Callery Road
Cranberry Township, PA 16066
E-mail: info@iaabc.org
www.iaabc.org

International Association of Canine Professionals (IACP)
P.O. Box 560156
Montverde, FL 34756-0156
Telephone: (877) THE-IACP
www.canineprofessionals.com

National Association of Dog Obedience Instructors (NADOI)
PMB 369
729 Grapevine Hwy.
Hurst, TX 76054-2085
www.nadoi.org

Veterinary and Health Resources

American Veterinary Dental Society (AVDS)
P.O. Box 803
Fayetteville, TN 37334
Telephone: (800) 332-AVDS
Fax: (931) 433-6289
E-mail: avds@avds-online.org
www.avds-online.org

Academy of Veterinary Homeopathy (AVH)
P.O. Box 232282
Leucadia, CA 92023-2282
Telephone/Fax: (866) 652-1590
www.theavh.com/contact/index.
php

American Academy of Veterinary Acupuncture (AAVA)
P.O. Box 1058
Glastonbury, CT 06033
Telephone: (860) 632-9911
Fax: (860) 659-8772
www.aava.org

American Animal Hospital Association (AAHA)
12575 W. Bayaud Ave.
Lakewood, CO 80228
Telephone: (303) 986-2800
Fax: (303) 986-1700
E-mail: info@aahanet.org
www.aahanet.org

American Kennel Club Canine Health Foundation (AKCCHF)
P.O. Box 37941
Raleigh, NC 27627-7941
Telephone: (888) 682-9696
E-mail: caninehealth@akcchf.org
www.akcchf.org

American College of Veterinary Internal Medicine (ACVIM)
1997 Wadsworth Blvd., Suite A
Lakewood, CO 80214-5293
Telephone: (800) 245-9081
Fax: (303) 231-0880
Email: ACVIM@ACVIM.org
www.acvim.org

American College of Veterinary Ophthalmologists (ACVO)
P.O. Box 1311
Meridian, ID 83860
Telephone: (208) 466-7624
Fax: (208) 466-7693
E-mail: office10@acvo.com
www.acvo.com

American Holistic Veterinary Medical Association (AHVMA)
2218 Old Emmorton Road
Bel Air, MD 21015
Telephone: (410) 569-0795
Fax: (410) 569-2346
E-mail: office@ahvma.org
www.ahvma.org

American Veterinary Medical Association (AVMA)
1931 North Meacham Road, Suite 100
Schaumburg, IL 60173-4360
Telephone: (800) 248-2862
Fax: (847) 925-1329
E-mail: avmainfo@avma.org
www.avma.org

ASPCA Animal Poison Control Center
Telephone: (888) 426-4435
www.aspca.org

British Veterinary Association (BVA)
7 Mansfield Street
London
United Kingdom
W1G 9NQ
Telephone: 0207 636 6541
Fax: 0207 908 6349
E-mail: bvahq@bva.co.uk
www.bva.co.uk

Canine Eye Registration Foundation (CERF)
VMDB/CERF
1248 Lynn Hall
625 Harrison St.
Purdue University
W. Lafayette, IN 47907-2026
Telephone: (765) 494-8179
E-mail: CERF@vmdb.org
www.vmdb.org/cerf.html

Orthopedic Foundation for Animals, Inc. (OFA)
2300 E. Nifong Blvd.
Columbia, MO 65201-3806
Phone: (800) 442-0418
E-mail: chic@offa.org
www.offa.org

US Food & Drug Administration's Center for Veterinary Medicine (CVM)
Communications Staff (CVM)
Food and Drug Administration
7519 Standish Place, HFV-12
Rockville, MD 20855
Telephone: (240) 276-9300
E-mail: ASKCVM@fda.hhs.gov
www.fda.gov/cvm/default.htm

Veterinary Pet Insurance
P.O. Box 2344
Brea, CA 92822-2344
Telephone: (800) USA-PETS
www.petinsurance.com

PUBLICATIONS

Books

Anderson, Teoti. *Puppy Care & Training.* Neptune City: TFH Publications, Inc., 2007.

Anderson, Teoti. *The Super Simple Guide to Housetraining.* Neptune City: TFH Publications, 2004.

Anne, Jonna, with Mary Straus. *The Healthy Dog Cookbook: 50 Nutritious and Delicious Recipes Your Dog Will Love.* UK: Ivy Press Limited, 2008.

Boneham, Sheila Webster, Ph.D. *The Multiple-Dog Family.* Neptune City: TFH Publications, Inc., 2009.

Boneham, Sheila Webster, Ph.D. *Training Your Dog for Life.* Neptune City: TFH Publications, Inc., 2008.

Dainty, Suellen. *50 Games to Play With Your Dog.* UK: Ivy Press Limited, 2007.

DeVito, Russell-Revesz, Fornino. *World Atlas of Dog Breeds, 6th Ed.* Neptune City: TFH Publications, Inc., 2009.

King, Trish. *Parenting Your Dog: Complete Care and Training for Every Life Stage.* Neptune City: TFH Publications, Inc., 2010.

Knueven, Doug, DVM. *The Holistic Health Guide for Dogs.* Neptune City: TFH Publications, Inc., 2008.

Morgan, Diane. *The Living Well Guide for Senior Dogs.* Neptune City: TFH Publications, Inc., 2007.

Magazines

AKC Family Dog
American Kennel Club
260 Madison Avenue
New York, NY 10016
Telephone: (800) 490-5675
E-mail: familydog@akc.org
www.akc.org/pubs/familydog

AKC Gazette
American Kennel Club
260 Madison Avenue
New York, NY 10016
Telephone: (800) 533-7323
E-mail: gazette@akc.org
www.akc.org/pubs/gazette

Dog Fancy
P.O. Box 6050
Mission Viejo, CA 92690-6050
Telephone: (800) 365-4421
E-mail: barkback@dogfancy.com
www.dogfancy.com

Dog & Kennel
Pet Publishing, Inc.
7-L Dundas Circle
Greensboro, NC 27407
Telephone: (336) 292-4047
Fax: (336) 292-4272
E-mail: info@petpublishing.com
www.dogandkennel.com

Dogs Monthly
Ascot House
High Street, Ascot,
Berkshire, SL5 7JG
United Kingdom
Telephone: 1344 628 269
Fax: 1344 622 771
E-mail: admin@rtc-associates.
freeserve.co.uk
www.corsini.co.uk/dogsmonthly

WEBSITES

Nylabone
www.nylabone.com

TFH Publications, Inc.
www.tfh.com

PHOTO CREDITS

ACKNOWLEDGMENTS

I would like to thank my mother, Dr. H. Judith Jarrell, and her aunt, Paula Mintz Gartman, for their initial editing. I would also like to thank my mentor Flo McDaniel, McMatt Australian Shepherds.

ABOUT THE AUTHOR

Elizabeth M. Jarrell of Bon Ami Australian Shepherds is a multiple, national award-winning

writer with national columns for different publications. She has won two Maxwell Awards from the Dog Writers' Association of America and three Arthur Awards from the Alliance of Purebred Dog Writers. Jarrell has campaigned her Australian Shepherds to the number-one, year-end standing in obedience and successfully placed with them in invitational competitions. She has also trialed her dogs to top-ten, year-end standings in agility and rally. She is a long-time member of the Australian Shepherd Club of America. She lives with her two Australian Shepherds, Sophia Maria and her son Kipling, in Maryland.

VETERINARY ADVISOR

Wayne Hunthausen, DVM, consulting veterinary editor and pet behavior consultant, is the director of Animal Behavior Consultations in the Kansas City area and currently serves on the Practitioner Board for *Veterinary Medicine* and the Behavior Advisory Board for *Veterinary Forum.*

BREEDER ADVISOR

Flo McDaniel has been involved in the sport of purebred dogs in 1974. She is a member of the Australian Shepherd Club of America (ASCA) since 1982 and has bred Australian Shepherds under the name McMatt Kennels since 1984. She owned 6 ASCA Hall of Fame dogs, many ASCA Champions, and 48 American Kennel Club (AKC) Champions. She has been the Education Chairperson for the United States Australian Shepherd Association (USASA), serves on USASA Breeder/Judge/Public Education Committee, and is an USASA Australian Shepherd Breed Mentor. She currently owns 5 Australian Shepherds.

NATURAL with added VITAMINS
Nutri Dent ®MD
Promotes Optimal Dental Health!

360° Design
Nylabone Cleaning Action!™

Dog's Love 'em! ™

AVAILABLE IN MULTIPLE SIZES AND FLAVORS.

Nylabone ®
Trusted For Over 40 Years

MADE IN THE USA